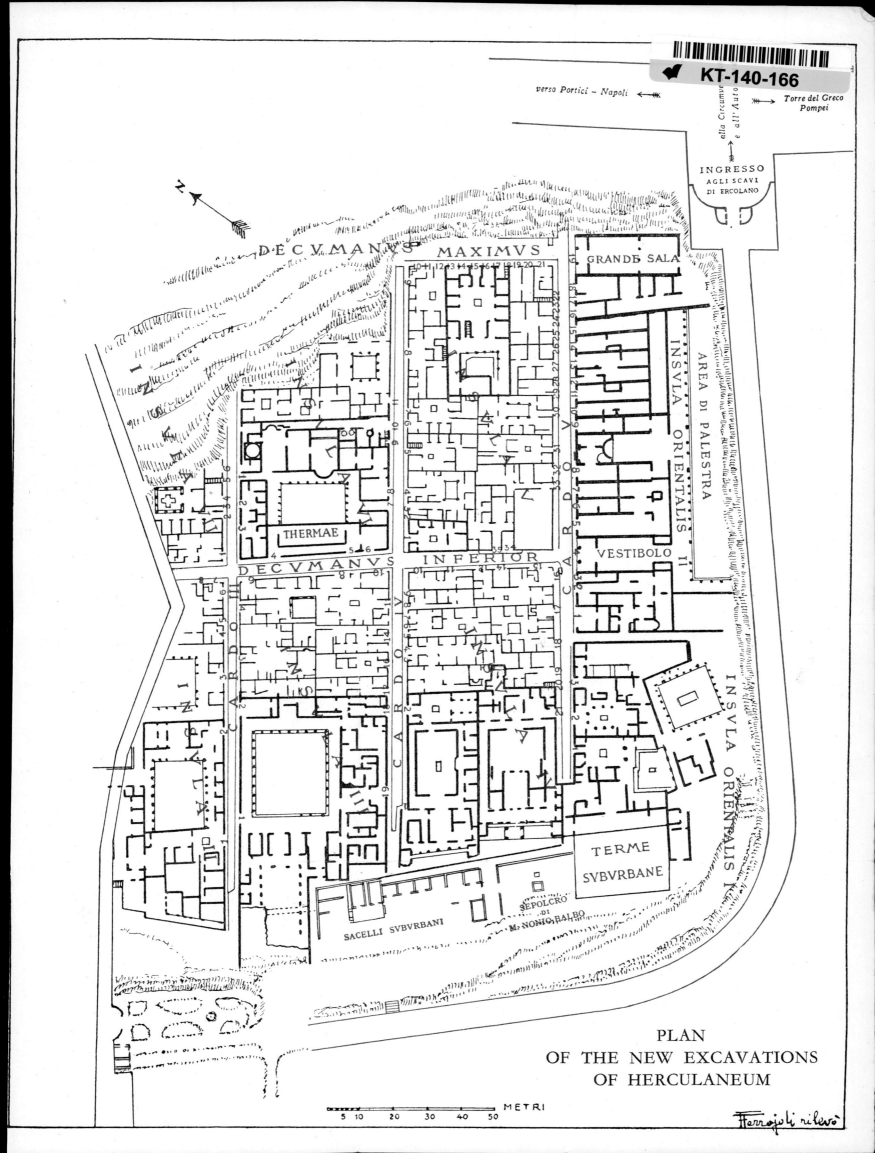

verso Portici – Napoli ←——

alla Circumve e all'Auto

——→ Torre del Greco
Pompei

INGRESSO
AGLI SCAVI
DI ERCOLANO

DECVMANVS MAXIMVS

GRANDE SALA

Z

THERMAE

DECVMANVS INFERIOR

INSVLA ORIENTALIS II

AREA DI PALESTRA

VESTIBOLO

INSVLA ORIENTALIS I

TERME
SVBVRBANE

SACELLI SVBVRBANI

SEPOLCRO
DI
M. NONIO BALBO

PLAN
OF THE NEW EXCAVATIONS
OF HERCULANEUM

METRI

5 10   20   30   40   50

Ferrajoli rilevò

MINISTERO DELLA PUBBLICA ISTRUZIONE

DIREZIONE GENERALE DELLE ANTICHITÀ E BELLE ARTI

GUIDE-BOOKS TO THE MUSEUMS AND MONUMENTS OF ITALY

AMEDEO MAIURI

Trans. by V. PRIESTLEY

HERCULANEUM

*(9 ILLUSTRATIONS IN THE TEXT
AND 72 PLATES)*

FIFTH REVISED AND UP TO DATE EDITION

ISTITUTO POLIGRAFICO DELLO STATO

LIBRERIA DELLO STATO

FOREWORD
TO THE FIRST AND SECOND EDITIONS

The first " Itinerary „ of the new excavations of Hercula-neum has reached completion nine years after the resumption of operations and four years after the publication of a larger book of a different nature (Ercolano, Novara 1932) likewise dedicated to the knowledge of the true face of the second city buried by Vesu-vius, such as it has been assuming since May 1927: i. e. when more than to inaugurate the resumption of excation works it was intended to conduct such works with firm and steadfast perseve-rance to their greatest possible completion.

This volume, then, though small and of modest pretentions, marks a period and a point in the new story of the Herculanean excavations, that within the space of a few years will be surpass-ed. But it has its own particular aim, that of putting on the path towards the understanding and love of Herculaneum those — and they are the majority of people — who only know through the mirage of the great discoveries of the past, to help them to know at last in reality, the disinterred city se dramatically and humanly alive, and to love il for that supreme beauty which expres-ses the struggles and the victory of the man who succeeds in tearing from the tremendous and ineluctable forces of the earth the mys-tery and the light of its faraway existence, broken but not van-quished, interrupted but not extinguished, by the most violent convulsion of the time.

A. M.

FOREWORD TO THE FOURTH EDITION

The progress of the excavations and the selling out of the IInd Italian and English editions rendered a revised and up to date reprinting of this little booklet necessary. It, of course, goes with the itinerary of Pompeii. In such way, the ever growing number of visitors to Herculaneum, notwithstanding the delay of the great publication of the new excavations caused by war circum-stances, will have the possibility to become acquainted with the new discoveries by means of this short but complete description.

A. M.

PRACTICAL INFORMATION

Herculaneum can be reached from Naples by the following means:

A) ELECTRIC RAILWAY (FERROVIA CIRCUMVESUVIANA), trains every half–hour, in 15 minutes by express and in about 25 minutes by ordinary trains, to the station of Pugliano (Resína). On leaving the station, the wide avenue to the left leads to the entrance of the Nuovi Scavi, which opens upon the Corso Ercolano of Resína (8–10 minutes).

B) By motor bus No. 155 from Piazza Municipio, Naples and by streetcar No. 55 from the stance near the Naples Central Station to the Entrance of the Excavations in respectively 20 minutes and 40 minutes. The route passes through the pictures que popular quarters of S. Giovanni a Teduccio and Resína.

C) Auto–Road: Naples–Herculaneum (4 ½ miles). Follow the Pugliano road downhill to the Circumvesuviana Railway level–crossing and thence proceed to the entrance of the Excavations. Private and touring cars are allowed access to the interior avenue leading from the main Entrance down to the esplanade from where the visit to the ruins commences.

D) FERROVIA DELLO STATO (STAZIONE CENTRALE): this line may be adopted for the tract Naples–Portici or Naples–Torre del Greco.

The Excavations are open to visitors from 9 a. m. to 4 p. m.

A complete visit may be made in 2 hours.

To visit the theatre it is necessary to be accompanied by a custodian.

HISTORICAL NOTE

*H*ERCULANEUM *was a small city of Campania, placed
four miles to the east of Naples along the lower slopes of
Vesuvius, which there formed an eminent promontory on
the coast–line, limited on both sides by the deeply channelled beds
of two torrents (Sisenna 4, fr. 53:* oppidum tumulo in excelso
loco propter mare, parvis moenibus, inter duos fluvios infra
Vesuvium collocatum); *in antiquity, as to–day, it was traversed
by the great coast–road that ran along the edge of the gulf by
Oplonte to Pompeii and thence to* Stabiae *and* Nuceria Alfaterna.
*The great eruption of mud–lava in 79 A. D. and that of fire–lava
in 163', which raised the ground–level morde than 20 metres,
levelled up the irregularities of the land and widened the littoral,
profoundly changed the physionomy of the region. Superimposed
over the greater part of the ancient city are the most populous
quarters of the modern Resina, and over its suburbs with their
many patrician villas rise the great Bourbon villas of Portici and
of the Favorita. Although numbered by Cicero* (De lege agr.,
II, 35, 96) *amongst the most important centres of Campania, it
owes its celebrity, like Pompeii, to the circumstances of art interment
and, above all, to the discoveries of works of rt which made of it in
the XVIII century the richest centre of archaelogical excavations.*

*According to the legend recounted by Dionysius of Halicarnas-
sus (I, 35), Herculaneum was founded by Hercules upon his return
from the fabulous journey in Iberia, and this, apart from the myth,
is enough to indicate it as a city of Greek origin, with a Greek
name: in fact, in the first mention of it in Theophastus (314 B. C.)
it appears under the name of* " Herácleion ,,.

*The monumental remains that have come to light up to the
present day tell us nothing of the most ancient period, and only
the new excavations have brought to light a part of the city wall,
the* parva moenia *recorded by Sisenna; only its ground–plan
(see below) by reason of its singular regularity and the orientation
of the* decumani *and the* cardines *certainly recalls the town–
plan of Naples, and on this basis it is possible to hold hat its real
and proper urban development was modelled on that of the great
neighbouring Greek city. The information given by Strabo
(V, 4, 8, p. 246) is only partly to be respected, where he assigns
the first domination of the city to the Oscans, then to the Tyrr-
henians and the Pelasgians, and finally to the Samnites. Certainly, as at Pompeii, there must first have been a small centre of*

5

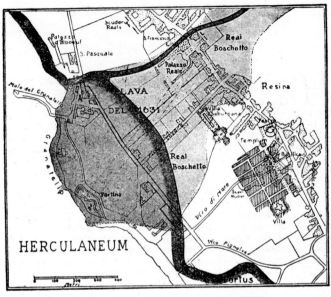

FIG. I — RESINA, PORTICI AND HERCULANEUM

the indigenous population before the development of the city, but
from the end of the VI century B. C. Herculaneum must have
fallen under the hegemony of the Greeks of Naples and Cumae,
who held sway over the whole Companian coast, from the rock of
Cumae and the island of Ischia to the extreme point of the Sor-
rentine peninsula (Capo Atenèo). It fell with Pompeii and all
the other cities of the Campania excepting Naples into the power
of the Samnites towards the end of the V century B. C.

It is uncertain whether in the second Samnite war Herculaneum followed the fortunes of Naples (326) or rather those of
Nuceria and Pompeii (307); it is certain, however, that in the last
rising of the Italic peoples against Rome, it rebelled as did Pompeii and Nola and was taken by force and vanquished by a legate
of Sulla (89 B. C.). From that time, having lost all autonomy,
it was transformed into a Roman municipality and perhaps it had,
like Pompeii and Sorrento, a colony of veterans from the Sullan
army. Of the Samnite period we have but few inscriptions in
the Oscan dialect, whilst of the Roman period the epigraphical

material, which has come to light in the excavations from time to time (Corp. Inscrip. lat., *X, 1401–77*) offers us the documentation of the principal municipal magistratures and of a college of augustales; there are also various honorary inscriptions referring to imperial and patricians of the city, and others relating to public monuments.

The earthquake of 62 A. D. must have had the same and perhaps not less grave consequences for Herculaneum as it had for Pompeii: both public and private edifices must have been seriously damaged, calling for radical restoration or complete rebuilding. To this there is the explicit testimony of the inscription (C. I. L., *X, 1406*) which records the restoration by Vespasian of the temple of the Mater Deum, after its ruin caused by the earthquake. But, as in the case of Pompeii, Herculaneum had not finished repairing the great damages of the catastrophe of the year 62 A. D. when it was overtaken by the extreme disaster, the eruption of 79 A. D.

THE ERUPTION

The circumstances of the burial of Herculaneum are very diverse from those of Pompeii and have been much discussed. Whilst a Pompeii there was a regular stratification of eruptive material due to the rain of ashes and fragments of lava transported by the wind, which was at the most 5 or 6 metres deep, upon Herculaneum there descended, swept down by the enormous volumes of water that always accompany great volcanic convulsions, a shapeless mass of erupted material which had previously collected around the crater and now rushed down the steep mountain side upon the city in the form of an immense torrent of mud, overturning and submerging all that stood in its path. First the villas lying above the city and then the city itself, all were submerged by this terrifying alluvion which, having invaded and filled up all spaces, totally transformed the aspect of the district. This mud-lava, that in its liquid state was able to penetrate into every void, now that it is solidified has assumed the appearance of a compact bank. It attains the hardness of tufa, and presents the characteristics of a tufoid formation (pappamonte), varying both in composition and in density according to the different flows of lava. The depth of the layer of earth thus accumulated above the buried city, including the vegetable stratum, varies from 12 to 20 metres or more.

Although this manner of burial has been placed in doubt by various authorities, who attribute the destruction of Herculaneum to the same rain of ashes and " lapilli ,, which interred Pompeii and the hardening of the earth to a simple precipitation of carbonate of calcium, the latter hypothesis conflicts with positive data yielded by the excavations, that is, by the fact that the upper parts of the scaena or stage building and of the cavea or auditorium of the theatre were found dismantled, with the greater part of the statuary overturned, various parts of the same piece of sculpture have been recovered at a great distance one from another along the streets transformed into otorrents, and vaulted localities have been found filled up to the top by the fluid mass which entered them through the skylights.

If the excavations have been and are still rendered extremely difficult by such circumstances, these have at the same time served to preserve the city from recuperations and rough–handling after the catastrophe, to preserve the upper parts of the edifices and, besides, thanks to the almost impermeables character of the earth, to preserve the wood, an element of far greater importance in ancient building than might be judged from the remains of other cities.

HISTORY OF THE DISCOVERIES

Although the memory of Herculaneum had not entirely disappeared from the local tradition (it is mentioned in Arcadia, by Sannazzaro, 1504) and although the possibility must not be excluded that from time to time the inhabitants of the superimposed Resina, when digging fondations and sinking wells, may have run into buildings of the buried city, the first important discovery of works of art is owed to the Austrian Prince d'Elboeuf, who, having ordered a well to be sunk in the wood of the Frati Alcantarini, encountered the wall of the stage–edifice of the theatre. From 1709 to 1716, d'Elboeuf was able to perpetrate with the greatest of ease the first great offence against the noblest and best–preserved monument of Herculaneum. The precious marble of the facings and of the architecture of the scaena were removed and a large group of statues, including the so–called " large ,, and " small ,, Herculanean statues of the Dresden Museum, was dispersed among the various museums. Regular excavations were begun on October 1st, 1738 and from that year the history of the exploration of Herculaneum may be divided into four periods:

I. 1738–1765: this was the most heroic and most fortunate period of excavation. Promoted and patronized by the Bourbon king, Charles III, the work was directed (excepting for a brief interruption from 1740–1745) by the Spanish military engineer Alcubierre, who had as his first assistant the Swiss architect Charles Weber, more diligent and accurate than Alcubierre himself, and, during the last year, Francesco La Vega. The excavation was effected by means of underground galleries, in the face of great *difficulties, overcome largely thanks to the merits of the local navvies (the so—called* cavamonti). *There were daily and weekly reports of the excavations but without, unfortunately, the necessary accompaniment of plans and elevations: those provided being too few and inadequate or now lost. The exploration of the Theatre was completed; there was reached, if not the Forum, at least one of the public edifices (the so—called Basilica); several temples were traced and lastly, between 1750 and 1765, the Villa of the Papyri was explored and all its fabulous treasure of sculpture and the library were recovered. Nevertheless, notwithstanding these results, little or nothing was learnt from these excavations of the city itself. Once the shafts for descent and ventilation were closed the galleries abandoned and refilled with earth from the excavations, all that remained was the general plan drawn up by La Vega and the one executed with great diligence by Charles Weber of the Villa of the Papyri.*

II. After an interval of 63 years, the excavations were resumed in 1828 with the praiseworthy intention of accomplishing them in the open, as had been done for some time at Pompeii, and they were continued without any great fervour until 1835, bringing to light with much toil part of two blocks of houses, including the peristyle of the so—called " House of Argo ,,.

III. Abandoned in 1855, the excavations were again taken up under the auspices of Victor Emanuel II in 1869, and pursued until 1875, but all that they brought to light was the beginning of two other insulae *and the south front of the* Thermae. *The work was arrested under the palisade of the houses of Resina and owing to the opposition of the land owners.*

IV. The attempt made in 1904 by the English archeologist Charles Waldstein to form an international organization for the excavation of Herculaneum was a failure. The work was resumed in 1927, in the charge of the Italian Government, with the determination to carry it out with the same continuity as that of Pompeii. The programme of the new operations is first of all to uncover a large part of the residential quarter of the city, gradually extending the excavations towards the zones less explored by the galleries of preceding excavators and, secondly, to explore the suburban areas, notoriously rich in patrician villas. The organization of the recent excavations and the results already obtained in these first few years have made Herculaneum an archaeological centre of te greatest and most vital interest for the study of ancient cities, formingaz precious aid and complement to Pompeii itself, and, finally, one of the most promising fields for the recovery of works of art.

THE CITY AND ITS MONUMENTS

WHILST the gradual, systematic disinterment of the residential quarter of Herculaneun is in progress, from the hore towards the mount and from east to west, we have, to give us an idea of the general plan of the city and of the character of its edifices, on the one hand the general plan traced by La Vega of the whole zone explored by the underground galleries, showing the simple outline of the *insulae,* and on the other the concrete, organic sight of the quarter already excavated and in course of excavation: the six southern *insulae,* besides the two great blocks of the eastern quarter.

The plan drawn up by La Vega (*v. fig. 2*) shows us a part only of the ancient city: eight *insulae* to the south of the great porticoed artery that is obviously to be recognized as the *decumanus maximus;* to the north of this artery there is a great rectangular edifice identified by some as the Forum area and by others again, more reasonably, as a *Basilica* or other public meeting–place; to the north–east there is the *Theatre* and next to it, in a free area, a *Temple* clearly indicated as such, being in the form of a temple on a podium with a cella preceded by a pronaos and an altar; further away, on the other side of a long, nar ow *insula* (it probably owes its form to the presence of the bed of a torrent which marked the confines of the city on that side), there spread out in the suburban district the great " Villa of the Papyri „; other scattered and isolated villas lay in the area of the present Royal Gardens of Portici, of which something was learnt during the work for the laying of the Palace foundations. To the east, there is a great square peristyle that was thought to be either a temple or a villa but which the new excavations have shown to be public building, that is the area of a large *palaestra.* Further to the south–east, about 150 metres from the limits marked by La Vega, the first sepulcres of the Herculanean necropolis are to be found, flanking as at Pompeii the great coast–road leading to Pompei, *Stabiae* and *Nuceria.* On the side of the city towards the sea, the houses, as is now clear from the new excavations, reached the extreme brow of the promontorv, following its margin with terraces and verandahs projecting over the shore, upported by heavy earth–filled walls, the empty spaces thus created in the slope of the land being utilized as

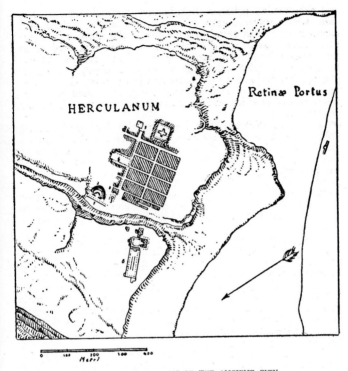

HERCULANUM

Retinæ Portus

FIG. 2 — GENERAL PLAN OF THE ANCIENT CITY

small store–cellars and other living rooms, now blocked up by the gigantic barrier of the wave of mud. The houses, however, did not, end at the edge of the promontory, but, as the excavations in course show (see page 65: *The suburban quarter*) extended outside the gates as far as the harbour and the shore, where they formed the maritime suburb of the city.

Thus, on three sides the confines of the city are sufficiently known but of the fourth side towards the mountain, occupied by the houses of Resína, little can be asserted, because we do not yet know how many of the edifices indicated along the slopes of Pugliano belong to the urban district and how many to the suburban. Since, however, the part already excavated and explored by galleries includes five *cardines* and two *decumani* which traverse each other at right angles, a third *decumanus* must almost certainly have run to the north across eight other *insulae*, as in the plan of *Neapolis*, making a total of sixteen *insulae*, besides the larger *insulae* of the eastern and western quarters (also calculable as another eight) and besides also the buildings along the coast and in the port, and the houses of the patrician families who dwelt with their numerous followings of servants and freedmen in villas in the surrounding countryside.

For some (Beloch), therefore, the city developed presumably within an area whose axes would measure about 370 metres by 320 (the third of Pompeii), but since the exact extension and configuration of the promontory upon which lay the residential quarters is still unknown to us, a precise calculation of the area can only be premature. The population alone may be calculated as being approximately, between city and suburb, from four to five thousand persons at the most (that is, a third, and perhaps less, of the population of Pompeii).

Herculaneum, with its *decumani* running like those of Naples parallel to the coast line, from north–west to south–east, and the *cardines* which lie from north–east to south–west, running down at right angles to the shore, certainly presents us with a much more regular plan than that of Pompeii, and, leaving apart the obscure and uncertain question of Etruscan influences upon the primitive plans of Campanian cities, it is undeniable that it mirrors both in orientation and distribution the lay–out of a city certainly Greek in origin and in plan, that is, Naples.

The steep acclivity of the land upon which the city, by means of artificial banking and levelling of the ground, distributed its edifices as upon so many successive terraces, reveals itself to us by the rapid inclination of the *cardines*, the gradual raising of the street pavements and by the different levels of the groundfloor in different parts of the same house. The abrupt elevation of the promontory above the shore is witnessed to, not only by the overhanging line of houses but also by the fact that all three *cardines*, when they reached the extreme edge of the hill with its sudden fall, descended rapidly down to the sea through archways, like the gates of a mediaeval citadel, recalling the rapid downward slope to the exit at the *Porta Marina* of Pompei (PL. XXXIX, *fig. 70*).

The roads excavated up to the present, paved not only with the characteristic trachytic Vesuvian stone still used in Naples and in the province, but also, as if to mark a greater nobility, with calcareous stone (*V cardo*), do not show either the deep cart–wheel ruts caused by heavy commercial traffic or the well–known stepping–stones from one pavement to the other, both to be seen at Pompeii. Here also there is the usual finer and better paving in front of the more important houses but the porticoed pavements, that run along the fronts of whole *insulae* or, as along the *decumanus*, on one at least of the fronts of a street from end to end, are more frequent at Herculaneum than at Pompeii (PL. VI, *figs. 11–12*).

Two public fountains at the points where the *decumani* cross the *V cardo*, and another where the *cardo IV* crosses the *decumanus maximus*, the presence of a water–tower at the cross–roads near the " Samnite House „ , of *nymphaea* and fountains in the courtyards and gardens of larger houses and of *fistulae* here and there, all indicate that the water–supply of Herculaneum underwent the same evolutions as that of Pompeii: from wells of latent water sunk to a little depth in the undersoil and the collection of rain–water the passage was made, in the Roman period, to the conveyance of water from more distant sources, with perhaps a branch–line of the Augustean aqueduct, which, coming from the upland of Serino, was the great water artery of the zone around Vesuvius (PL. III, *fig. 6*). The substitution was not complete, however, as it was at Pompeii, and it is a singular fact that the public Baths were supplied up to the last by water drawn up from a well (s. THERMAE).

Until the new excavations shall have reached and brought to light the Forum quarter, little can be said of the monumental public buildings, civil and religious, of Herculaneum and still less of the structural and architectural development from the Samnite period to the time of the Romans. The *Thermae* (p. 35) and the *Theatre* (see p. 67) seem both to belong to the first Augustan period, with later decorative embellishment during the Claudian and Flavian periods. The most important of the other public edifices brought to light during the old excavations is the so–called *Basilica*: this, together with the Theatre, has restored to us the most important nucleus of works of art in the city area. In sculpture, it has yielded the equestrian statues and the series of honorary statues to the Balbus family and the fragments, not yet all recuperated, of the large bronze quadriga which seems must have surmounted the entrance *propylon*. In painting, there have been recovered some of the best examples of ancient art, such as the *Hercules and Telephus, Theseus victorious, Cheiron and Achilles, Marsyas and Olympus,* which decorated the apses of the hall. Only one of the buildings baptised by the Bourbon excavators as

Temples seems to be so for certain, the one that is marked at the side of the Theatre on La Vega's plan. The others in the extreme eastern quarter of the city seem rather to be grandiose vestibules to a public *palaestra*, to judge by recent excavations.

CONSTRUCTIONAL FORMS AND DEVELOPMENT IN HERCULANEUM

The true image of Herculaneum is to be drawn more from its private than from its public buildings, more from the sight of the quarter already disinterred, with its elegant residences and poorer dwellings, than from the history of its underground discoveries. It is to be learnt by wandering again and again up and down the first street with their paving intact, visiting again and again the ancient cross–roads which have reemerged mysteriously from that tremendous regurgitation of the earth. And even the most inattentive eye immediately gathers the profound difference between the two Vesuvian cities drawn together by the same lot. There are not the obtrusive notices on the walls which invade every corner of Pompeii (PL. VII, *figs. 13–14*). The shops and *tabernae*, though often large and well–furnished in the busier parts of the town, do not reveal that absolute predomination of the commercial classes witnessed to in almost all parts of Pompeii, and there are few industrial workshops and laboratories. On the other hand the various handicrafts and minor arts must have been more developed here: that of the mosaic–worker, who produced the precious revetments, that of the marble worker who exe-cuted the intarsia–work in polychrome marbles, a luxury almost common in Herculanean houses, that of the cabinet–maker and wood–carver who made artistic furniture such as beds, tables, cupboards and little shrines. The favourite occupation of the common people, however, must have been fishing, because great quantities of nets, hooks, ropes and fishing utensils have been found in both the old and new excavations.

Contrary to that which might have been expected, it is clear even from the few *insulae* which have so far been completely excavat d that the Herculanean house is more evolved, freer and more advanced on the way towards the adoption of new forms end new types than the Pompeian house appears to be. Even at Pompeii the old schemes of the Italic dwelling were in a state of gradual evolution towards new forms imposed by the constant development of town life, that is, there was the atrophism of the old patrician house, the division of the ancient *domus* into commercial offices and apartments to let and the development of the upper floors in order to gain in height that which it was impossible to have in extension. At Herculaneum the process seems to have been still more rapid, because of a more radical transformation of the Italic and Hellenistic house under the influence on the one hand of the practical Roman spirit and on the other under the still more direct and profound influence which a city like Naples. crowded by reason of the crisis of urbanism within her old Grek walls, must have exercised over the neighbouring Herculaneum.

Nevertheless, we have at Herculaneum houses of a type still definitely Samnite, that were daringly heightened in the Roman period by the addition of another floor above a roof of the compluviate type (" Casa del tramezzo di legno „); there are house of the middle classes that have abandoned every tie which bound them to the traditional plan of the Italic house, the atrium being substitued by the courtyard of the modern house for the provision of light and ventilation, and the primitive privacy of the *domus* was substitued by the cohabitation of a number of tenants. There are richer houses where the Hellenistic type of portico has been completely transformed into a closed portico with windows, like a wide corridor; finally, there is the large block of the oriental quarter (*Insula orientalis II*), which offers us the type of house of the imperial period, with many storeys and apartments, previously known to us only at Ostia.

Although only a small part of the city has been so far disinterred, the private edifices of Herculaneum present us even now with an unsuspected variety of types and forms for the study of that which remains the essential problem in the history of civilization: the origin and development of the house. As the excavations spread out little by little and lead us further into the heart of the city towards the Forum, the types of Herculanean dwellings are continually enriched by new forms and reflect ever more clearly the class, life and habits of their inhabitants. In a city that did not undergo, as did Pompeii, the levelling current of industry and commerce, where the principal occupation was navigation and fishing, the contrasti between rich and elegant houses and popular habitations is stronger and more profound. The greater part of the area of an *insula* is occupied by two or three rich and spacious houses, whilst the rest is taken up by more modest dwellings, huddled in narrow spaces and obliged to add upper storeys. Often these latter, usually with a shop attached, succeed in insinuating themselves and extending themselves between the surrounding houses at the expense of pre—existing noble residences, according to the more or less prosperous state of their owner.

Since the city, placed above its mirroring sea, was created above all for the enjoyment of the panorama and the sea breezes, the wealthiest and most beautiful houses spread themselves out like a garland along the brow of the promontory, exposed towards the sea, with many open verandahs, terraces, belvederes and rooms for the siesta. It can be said that the houses of this type discovered up to the present (the " Casa dell'atrio a mosaico ,, , the " Casa dei Cervi ,, , the " Casa della Gemma ,, and the " Casa del rilievo di Telefo ,,) reassume in themselves all the character, the taste and the spirit of the upper classes of Herculaneum in the last decades of the city's life. They are rich and sumptuous, with precious pavements of polychrome marbles according to the fashion and taste of the Neronian and Flavian periods and fine painted decoration, and are adorned by works of art, but they were constructed above all to look out over the enchanting view of the gulf. They rise up and extend themselves upon the massive bastions of the scarped counteforts down the steep slope of the underlying lava. Along this front are disposed loggias, terraces, hanging gardens and small, elegant alcoves for the hours of repose in the daytime (*cubicula diurna*), for those beatific hours of the afternoon siesta dedicated with pleasant readings and amicable conversation to that *otium* which the Romans knew not how to separate from the delectation of the spirit and the mind. Along the axes of those verandahs and those loggias run porticoes and internal corridors, in order to carry the reflection of the distant glare of sky and sea into the most secret and intimate corners of the house. In short, the whole habitation is orientated panoramically towards the prospect of the gulf and transforms itself, so far as space permits, from a town house into a villa. Looking towards this extremity of the city from the sea, the throng of houses placed one above the other upon the rapid mountainslope must have seemed to terminate in an aerial girdle of porticoes and verandahs (PL. III, *fig. 5*).

By the side of these distinguished abodes, Herculaneum has preserved to us the type of modest and economic dwelling occupied by artisans' families, divided into small separate flats, of which we have one example, amongst many, that is insuperable for the miraculous preservation of its lowly technique of wooden frame—work and trellising, and for its humble, living, vibrating humanity (see " Casa a graticcio ,, , p. 30).

The Herculanean house presents itself to us with a spirit all its own of life and intimacy. The more perfect state of preservation of the upper storeys and, above all, the preservation of the wooden framework of the house, that is, of the rafters of the attics and roof, the window—frames, the doors, stairs, partitions, beds and commoner utensils, all tend to give a sense of familiarity and completeness to the habitation which it is not always possible to have at Pompeii. Thus, by means of patient and delicate work of restoration and protection, it is possible still to maintain and replace in their proper positions robust upporting architraves and the beams of ceilling and even more: it is possible to make the doors swing again on their ancient hinges and to mount up to the upper floors by means of the original wooden stairs, protected by sheets of plate—glass.

But in order to penetrate this interior spirit of the place, it is necessary to examine houses both rich and poor, to rove amongst shops and private houses, to get to know the ordinary objects of daily use, to pause in the most secret corners of a house and to remain awhile in repose on the rough threshold of a doorway or of a backshop.

A buried city is not excavated solely for the sake of rare and beautiful things to be looked at one by one; with such partiality, interest and curiosity would soon be exhausted. It is rather that the ancient cities which rise again have, like the historical cities that take on a new lease of life, a physiognomy, a visage, a spirit of their own, which the spirit of the visitor perceives and relives. Herculaneum is reassuming more and more its old face and spirit as the excavations gradually spread out and streets and houses, instead of being interrupted and fragmentary, subordinate and coordinate themselves into a quarter, into the general plan of a residential district, with its characteristic aspect and local colour. The choice public which visits it observes this slow breathing of the city gradually coming to life again; they are enraptured and go away inebriated, as it were, by it.

Herculaneum exalts the visitor by the wonderful humanity of its house, by that which it presents of the unexpected and unsuspected in true aspects of life, by that which is humble, profoundly human and intimate in the innermost corners of the abode: the bedroom, with its wooden bed and the little marble table close to it; the siesta—room with the more elaborate bed for daytime repose, inlaid with precious woods; the larder with the last crust saved from the day before by the careful housewife; the little storeroom with the wooden cupboard that served a double purpose, as a tabernacle for the images of the Lares and as a secret home for the necklaces and other precious objects belonging to the mistress of the house and, finally the presence of the most ancient symbol of the Cross, that is of a monument of exceptional interest for the primitive history of Christianity (*p. 48*).

The lack of human victims, which make the sight of Pompeian houses so dramatic, is neither felt nor lamented in these light, tranquil habitations, still prepared and waiting to receive their tenants and their friends; the sight of death would be too distressing and unpleasant in the midst of such pulsing life. These houses were abandoned with all their domestic accessories by their owners intent on flight as soon as possible in the direction of Naples or the sea, and we re–enter them, with our dolorous experience of survivers, after little less than two thousand years, wishful to pick up the threads again of that old way of life.

THE NEW EXCAVATIONS

The excavations were resumed at the point where they had been abandoned and closed by powerful buttressed walls in 1875 (PL. I, *fig. 2*). The first part to be worked was the whole of the eastern front, the zone of the ancient city which is completely free from modern buildings. The excavations extended from there towards the mount, where in order to be able to reach at least the chief *decumanus* and the central residential quarter it is necessary to proceed to the partial demolition of humble houses of one of the most populous quarters of Resína.

The new excavations of Herculaneum, at the beginning of the XVIIIth year from their commencement, have completely disinterred three great blocks of the southern quarter of the city (*insulae III, IV and V*), completed the excavation of the *Thermae* (previously only the *palaestra* was known), uncovered two grandiose blocks of the eastern quarter, of which the larger overlooks the area of a vast *palaestra* flanked by porticoes; besides, in these last years has been begun the disinterment of the suburban area outside the city walls and the southern gates. That is to say, in fifteen years, an area has been excavated that is, between streets and edifices, three times the size of that brought to light in the eastern quarter with such lean results (no house was ever isolated in its entirety) during fifty years of fervour and indecision, abandonment and rexmption between 1825 and 1875 (PL. II, *figs. 3–4*).

After the complete disinterment of the buildings of the *insula orientalis*, it will be possible in following years to renew the excavation of *insulae V–VI*, in order to let them take again their normal position along the *decumanus maximus*, and afterwards to explore the suburban area and the region of the necropolis, where doubtless other patrician villas have in store for us the most coveted fruits in the form of sculpture and other works of art, besides further collections of papyri.

TECHNIQUE AND ADMINISTRATION
OF THE EXCAVATIONS

If the excavation of Pompeii calls for particular care and skill on the part of workmen and craftsmen and for a sense of art and good judgement on that of the directors, in order to weld into an harmonic whole the different works of disinterment, protection, restoration and renovation so that simple digging suffices to restore to us that admirable document of life which is the ancient house. But the uncovering of Herculaneum presents us with far graver problems and more arduous difficulties to be overcome before the work of the excavator passes over into the slower and more exacting work of recovery, recomposition and protection of the remaining structural, architectural and decorative elements of a city buried and custodied in a stratum of solidified mud sometimes as hard as tufa. It is necessary to separate from the hard compact mass, from the tenacious grip of the cast of mud, cracked and fallen walls, plaster and stuccoes detached from the poor walls rotted by the perennial dampness of the earth, fallen rafters, slight woodwork partitions, often trellised, and finally, all the various small furnishings of a house: not only those in bronze, iron and terracotta, but also those in wood, bone and glass, not to mention the egg–shells still to be found in the closed larder of the house and the fine fibres of the papyrus rolls to the wax tablets that preserve receipts and private accounts, and sometimes bear the traces of the *atramentum* of the writing upon them (PL. IV, *figs. 7–8*).

Besides the hardness and the depth of the overlying earth which constitute, in those parts where the underground excavations were not conducted, exceptionally favourable conditions for the preservation of works of art and other fittings there are other and greater difficulties caused by the underground galleries opened by the Bourbon excavators everywhere, in every direction, even in the upper stories of the buildings, in a period when the only aim of excavation was to draw works of art from the bowels of the undersoil without any respect for the structure of the buildings, condemned to remain buried for ever (PL. V, *figs. 9–10*).

The opening of these underground galleries across roads, walls of houses and public edifices, together with the refilling of them with the earth previously excavated, has meant that most walls are found perforated in the lower parts and often only sustained by the mere vice of the solidified mud. There is a succession of perforated doors, pavements and lofts, ruined vaults, and of jambs and pilasters broken, crushed or completely overthrown by the weight above them or because of the removal of the earth against which they formerly leant. A typical example of the consequences of this wretched system of excavation is the fallen vault of the great ante–chamber to the immense peristyle of the *insula orientalis* (erroneously believed to be the Temple of the *Mater Deum*), caused by the tunnelling of La Vega.

The presence, then, of these " cunicoli ,, in the area which necessarily had to be explored first of all has rendered the disinterment of all the buildings extremely complex and difficult. Here it is not always possible to follow the old traditional rule of stratigraphic excavation : underbuilding is necessary unsteady walls have to be strengthened at the base, fearful breaches have to be filled in before freeing the upper storeys from their earthen covering and whole walls of frescoes have to be recomposed from the minute fragments to which they were reduced by the destructive fury of the dark, unguided tunnelling of the navvies, the *cavamonti*. It often happens, therefore, that in a nobly painted room the upper part of this decoration is preserved to a notable height, whilst the lower section is entirely missing and sometimes the upper floor of a house is in better condition that the ground floor. In view of the fact that the houses of Herculaneum are sometimes preserved to a quite considerable height, everyone can appreciate the amount of diligent work and skilful ingenious expediences, drawn from the century–old tradition of Neapolitan workers, required to bring about the disinterment of one edifice and its final arrangement, in such manner as to secure and guarantee all its structural and decorative material, ranging from the wall structures to the friable carbonized wood, from the iron gratings of a window to the shreds of vegetable fibre which had once been the counterpane of a bed.

Here, too, as at Pompeii, the most scrupulous respect for antiquity guides both excavator and restorer, so that in the masonry all the restorations, whether in the form of supports at the base of the wall or the replacement of missing parts or the due protection along the top, are clearly distinguishable to all who have even the slightest knowledge of the matter.

DESCRIPTION OF THE LOCALITY

A great avenue leads down from the new entrance on *Corso Ercolano* of Resína along the south front of the excavation, to the point where the ordered, intense life of the excavation-yard is in full swing. From the vantage-point of the avenue a bird's-eye view of the disinterred quarters of the city is obtained, and the height of the steep slopes and modern houses which overhang it and hem it in is a gauge of the grandiosity of the completed work and that which is to follow. The cut made in the hard, compact bank of the mud-flow by means of wedges, levers and picks, with the traditional ability of the *cavamonti*, stands clearly out lined around the area of excavation. At the point where the archaeological stratum commences with the appearance of walls, the rude work of the navvy is succeeded by that of the practised excavator and, from time to time, the action of the mechanical shovel operated and guided by the hands of the digger takes the place of the blows of the pickaxe. Everywhere along the excavation trenches are to be seen the mouths of the subterranean galleries which pierce the tufoid bank in all directions, refilled with softer earth either by the old excavators or by soil that has filtered down through the old wells of descent.

The present *Itinerary* is a brief but complete description of all the edifices within the zone of the new excavations, with the exception of the Theatre, which lies outside the said zone (s. p. 61). For the visitor who has less time at his disposal, the following itinerary is suggested:

" Casa d'Argo ,, (p. 24); " Casa detta dell'Albergo ,, (p. 26); " Casa dell'Atrio a mosaico ,, (p. 27); " Casa a graticcio ,, (p. 32); " Casa del tramezzo di legno ,, (p. 33); " Thermae ,, (p. 37); " Casa sannitica ,, (p. 42); " Casa del mosaico di Nettuno ed Anfitrite ,, (p. 44); " Casa del Bicentenario ,, (p. 47); " Palestra ,, (p. 55); " Casa del rilievo di Telefo ,, (è. 65); " Casa della Gemma (p. 65); " Casa dei Cervi ,, (p. 61).

(N. B. – *Edifices, houses and shops are marked with the number of the Insula and that of their entrance, the entrance numbering starting, where it is possible, on the west side of each Insula. Houses and shops of insulae not yet completely excavated are provisionally distinguished by a number or a letter).*

OLD EXCAVATIONS

INSULA II

CASA DI ARISTIDE (*Insula II, n. 1*). – This house was erroneously so-named by the old excavators and the ciceroni of the place after the discovery of the statue of Æschines from the " Villa dei Papyri ,,. It is the first habitation to be passed when ascending the *III cardo* from the south front of the *insula*. Part of the house (the *atrium* which opens directly upon the street without *fauces* but with a porch outside) and the back quarters are constructed upon the extreme brow of the hill; all the rest, which advances and projects outwards over the lowest and steepest slope of the promontory is supported upon robust vaulted constructions that form a powerful supporting bastion with concrete walls sometimes three metres thick, faced externally with brick and internally with *opus reticulatum*. Little remains that is intelligible of the original plan and decoration of the house after the devastation and alteration which it suffered because of the underground passages cut across it and the arbitary restorations made at the time, but its subterranean areas are imposing, down to the lower floor of the store–rooms looking seawards. These latter are to be reached by stairs from the house or by following the street pavement, covered by a penthouse and a vault, the only outlet of the *cardo* towards the outer world.

CASA D'ARGO (*Insula II, n. 2*). – The name of this house is derived from a charming painting of *Io guarded by Argus,* of which no trace now remains upon the wall of the great room ripening upon the peristyle. It was the most beautiful of the oouses brought to light by the old excavations during the pehod from 1828–1835. It is undoubtedly a noble example of the patrician abodes of Herculaneum but the only parts of it uncovered in that period were the eastern quarter with a stately but evidently secondary entrance from the *III cardo* and some of the ground–floor and cellar rooms along the southern front; the rest of the dwelling is still buried beneath the modern " Vico a Mare ,, for the rest of the extent of the *insula*. The ample galleries to be seen on the edge of the excavated area, under the bank of the road, are the old tunnels, now closed, that led across the " House of Argus ,, to the " Villa suburbana dei Papiri ,,.

The magnificence and distinction of the habitation are at once to be gathered from its long street–wall in *opus reti-*

culatum in good condition from the surviving pilastres of the entrance porch and, above all, from the great perystile around three sides of the garden, composed of columns and half–columns against pilasters of tufa and brick, finely stuccoed (8 columns and pilasters on the long sides, 4 columns and pilasters on the short sides), upon which opened a large *triclinium* and the minor rooms of the north side (PL. VIII, *fig. 15*). Around the portico on the upper floor were living rooms and storerooms for the deposit of a large quantity of cereals and other comestibles, supported by stout beams and projecting over the pavement on the street side. Nothing however, remains of this wonderful whole of a private dwelling and its domestic furniture, since at the time of its excavation those adequate steps for its preservation were not taken which only the perfected technique of the new excavations can offer. Beyond the first great peristyle towards the east there lay another with stuccoed brick columns (the south–east corner of it is to be seen, the rest is buried under the mud–flow); this must have been followed by the whole *atrium* quarter back to the principal exit on the west *cardo* of the *insula*. Thus we can say that the " Casa d'Argo ,, together with the other houses on the west side of the residential district, will form one of the goals of future Herculanean explorations, when, the work on the eastern and northern fronts being finished the march in the direction of the " Villa suburbana dei Papiri ,, will once more be taken up.

CASA DETTA DEL GENIO (*Insula II, n. 3*). – This house was poerctically so–named from the little *Cupid* or winged *Genius* discovered in it, once part of a marble candelabrum. Here too, we see only a small part of a large noble habitation which, with its living quarters, must also have reached back to the west *cardo*. The 1828 excavations disinterred only the secondary entrance (preceded by a porch, as in the case of the " Casa d'Argo ,,) and part of a vast peristyle with a few rooms on either side of the entrance. In the centre of the garden there is the rectangular fountain–basin, curved at its two extremities; it must once have been adorned along its edge by little decorative sculptures, as is indicated by the two remaining stelae.

HOUSE AND SHOPS (*Insula II, n. 4–8*). – After the three more or less ample and distinguished dwellings of the " Casa d'Aristide ,, , the " Casa d'Argo ,, and the " Casa del Genio ,, the rest of the *insula*, in closer contact with the artery of the lower *decumanus*, is occupied by more modest houses of *mercatores* and by shops. There is a large *thermopolium*, with two back–shops and an elaborate counter faced with marble

23

fragments; it opens with two large doorways upon the corner formed by the *cardo* and the *decumanus,* in a manner we shall have occasion to note at other cross—roads of the same street.

INSULA VII

HABITATIONS OF *Insula VII.* – The preceding excavators, owing to the lack of space and the overhead buildings only succeeded in disinterring the extreme south—west corner of this *insula,* with part of two habitations (*n. 1–2*) and two shops (*n. 3–4*). The first, which overlooks the *decumanus,* witnesses to the well—developed upper storey by the numerous windows and the terracotta pipes placed in the thickness of the walls. The second house, *n. 3,* improperly called that of *Galba* (from a bust of this emperor found in the street in front), was a dwelling of the patrician type which perhaps also extended across the whole *insula* from one *cardo* to the other. In the interior, there opens down one side of the peristyle a series of little rooms innocent of all decoration and on the other side a large exedra that still preserves part of its decoration in the IV architectural style. The republican peristyle ois of particular interest, with its late—Doric tufa columns; these were later faced with coloured stucco and, at the same time, the intercolumnar space were closed by a podium. In the centre there is a cruciform basin faced with marble. The other columns now set in the walls of the south—side *cubicula* suggest a colonnade formated by a double order of columns, a unique example in the private architecture of Pompei and Herculaneum (PL. VIII, *fig. 16*). The following rooms (*n. 5–6*) are doorways leading to the upper floor of a dwelling belonging to the so—named " Casa di Galba ".

NEW EXCAVATIONS

INSULAE III AND IV ALONG THE CARDO IV

Returning to the lower end of the street, we enter the:

CASA DEL COSIDDETTO ALBERGO (*Insula III, n. 1?*). – This was the most spsacious and, perhaps, also the richest abode of the whole southern quarter of the city, occupying three-fifths at least of the entire area of *insula III,* much more than the space occupied by the other five or six dwellings of the *insula* taken altogether. In the preceding excavations, the whole of the side overlooking the *III cardo* was brought to light, and perhaps the grandiosity of its proportions or some particular find led to the false conviction that the house were an " hotel ,, , or, as was later thought for some time because of the pilastered terrace on the south side, a Basilica. Instead, its plan, though complex, reveals all the characteristics of a private dwelling, created for the double enjoyment of the wide panorama of the gulf and of the large garden with shady colonnades towards the inner part of the habitation; it advances with its great terrace to the extreme brow of the hill and under the terrace were opened other living rooms, cool spots and belvederes, also mistakenly believed at one time to be an underground sanctuary.

Unfortunately, it is this edifice, amongst all those excavated up to date, that has come down to us in the worst condition, not only because of the damage wrought by the eruption (which would seem here to have uprooted and overthrown the greater part of the walls in the fury of the muddy alluvion) and by the galleries of the Bourbon excavators but more particularly by reason of the many alterations that it underwent in antiquity, especially the last transformation partly effected and partly under way at the time of the catastrophe. Many details betray the change from a patrician house into a dwelling of a more commercial and utilitarian character: the detachment and conversion of a whole wing of the south side into a small self-contained dwelling (*n. 18*); the conversion of one of the large portico rooms into a shop (*n. 2*); the abandoned state in which was found the private bath constructed during the good Augustan period; the presence of a courtyard and its sorrounding rooms that call to mind a workshop rather than rustic servants' quarters. In short, even at Herculaneum, as at Pompeii, there is the gradual rise and invasion of the commercial classes, which succeed in supplanting the old and impoverished patrician class in the richest town houses. But spoilt and mutilated as it has come down to us, this house constitutes one of the most singular and instructive constructions of a private character of antiquity, both for the complexity of its plan and for the greater use here than else–where of corridors for the disengagement one from another of the various groups of rooms.

The main entrance to the house is at *n. 19* on the *IV cardo* and there is a secondary entrance at *n. 1* on the *III cardo*. The habitation may be divided into the following parts: *A*) The *atrium* quarter, with the private bath (on the right), which still retains signs of its primitive destination in its II style decoration and in the pavement, and numerous rooms on the left:

some of these still preserve the original pavement in *opus signi-num* with a delicate decoration in white tesserae; *B*) the peristyle quarter, with the large sunken garden below the level of the portico, where the carbonized trunk of a pear tree was found; *C*) the quarter of the great porticoed terrace with the large reception room and lesser *cubicula*; *D*) the quarter of the lower floor and the subterranean rooms; only the staircase with the long corridor leading down to them has so far been excavated.

Let us visit the " Casa dell'atrio a mosaico ,, on the opposite side of the road, Insula IV, n. 1–2, before going further.

CASA DELL'ATRIO A MOSAICO (*Insula IV, n. 1–2*). – This house takes it name from the singular mosaic chess–board decoration of the *atrium*; it is one of the most beautiful panor-amic houses of the southern quarter of the city. It may be divided into two distinct parts: the entrance, the *atrium* and the *tablinum* open normally along the east–west axis of the *insula*; the portico, with its reception rooms and living rooms on the terraces overlooking the sea, lies from north to south, a disposition common to all the rich and beautiful houses facing the lovely, wide, far–reaching view over the gulf. The diffe-rent ground–levels of the two quarters are due to the natural slope in the ground (*fig. 3*).

The mosaic pavements in the *fauces* and the *atrium* are intact: the one in the *fauces* is in squares with decorative em-blems and recalls the divisions and motifs of a carpet, while the one in the *atrium* has a simple geometrical design with large black and white rectangles. The marble *impluvium* tank, perhaps because of the irregular conformation of the roof, appears to be out of line. The undulation of the pavement is due to the yielding of the ground beneath the enormous weight of the eruptive mass. The form of the *tablinum* is curious, closed at the end, with partitions of pilasters and windows above the pilasters; the result is three aisles, a wider and higher one in the centre flanked by two minor lower ones on either side, which constitute almost the plan of a basilica in embryo (PL. XXV, *fig. 45*).

A windowed portico, that is, of the type with the inter-columnar spaces walled in and windows cut into them, and two entrances into the garden (there are here copious remains of carbonized wood) forms a convenient means of communication between the two parts of the house, sheltered from inclemencies of the weather and passing atmospheric disturbances (PL. XXV, *fig. 46*; XXVI, *fig. 47*; XXVIII, *fig. 50*). Along the east side, where the portico contracts into a narrow corridor protected

FIG. 3 – CASA DELL'ATRIO A MOSAICO

by glass (there remain clear traces of the sashes), there lies a series of small rooms. There are four pleasant *cubicula* with red walls, and the ceilings largely recomposed; these lie two on either side of a beautiful central exedra with slender architecture vaguely indicated on the azure ground of the walls, and little landscape paintings of a mythological character inserted on either hand: the *Punishment of Dirce* and *Diana bathing*. (PL. XXVII, *figs. 48–49*). From this slightly elevated *exedra* was enjoyed the view and the freshness of the garden enlivened by the jet of water rising from a marble basin.

The real living quarters of the house are reached from the south wing of the portico; in the centre lies the grandiose *triclinium*, with remains of the original marble pavement and wall–painting, flanked by other smaller rooms (in the one to the left is to be noted the extremely fine decoration on a white ground). All the rooms look out upon the covered colonnade and upon an underlying, narrower, open terrace. On either side of the colonnade opens a small elegant room for the siesta and from which to enjoy the view: these, from their form and their exposure, are to be identified with the *cubicula diurna* of Roman patrician houses and villas.

Continuing up the left side of the IV cardo:

CASA DELL'ERMA IN BRONZO (*Insula III, n. 16*). – This house, tiny and humble as it is, with a long, narrow ground-plan, preserved up to the end the original structure and characteristics of the Samnite house, recognizable above all in the employment of *opus quadratum* in tufa for the door–jambs of the portal, the doorways opening upon the *atrium* and the elegantly shaped *impluvium* basin. Lack of space later compelled the reduction and simplification of the original plan of the Samnite dwelling, and the abolition of the rooms along the two sides of the *atrium*. Internally, besides the two rooms near the *fauces*, there are at the other end of the *atrium* a small *tablinum*, an open light–well and a large room, perhaps the *triclinium*, with some remains of the decoration. Before one of the antae of the *tablinum* there is a vigorous portrait in bronze with coarse features, of local art and work–manship, almost certainly that of the owner of the house. The living–rooms were undoubtedly on the upper floor, reached by the stairs to be found in the simple blind corridor to the right of the *tablinum*, in the corner of which there is also a well–head (PL. X, *fig.* 19).

Facing there opens the entrance to the

CASA DELL'ALCOVA (*Insula IV, n. 3–4*). – The street façade in *opus reticulatum*, broken by various windows and by small square openings with iron gratings, shows the remains of the long, overhanging gallery which ran along on the level of the first floor (PL. IX, *fig. 18*). The smaller of the two entrances, that at *n. 4*, led by a straight flight of stairs to the rooms overlooking the street on the upper floor.

The whole of the habitation on the ground floor is formed by the rectangles of two adjoining houses originally independent and later thrown into one, with a large communicating door in the vestibule of the main entrance. Each of the two parts of the house has its own distinct character: the dwelling which unfolds along the axis of the *fauces*, with a very long, narrow ground–plan, is extremely rustic and modest, with the exception of the vestibule and one or two other rooms with the remains of decoration, whilst the house on a lower level to the south is of a far more distinguished type and must have formed the actual dwelling quarters of the master of the house. There is a covered *atrium*, with a black tessellated pavement with polychrome rhombi in *opus sectile*, upon which opens (on the street side) a room with two couches in wood and the upper part of the walls richly painted in the most sumptuous manner of the Pompeian IV style. On the other side of the *atrium* there is a much larger *triclinium* and reception room, where unfortunately but little remains of the richmarble pavement with polychrome squares. A long corridor with fine tessellation of the time of Augustus leads to a secluded spot for repose, an alcove (in the form of an apsed room like a *calidarium*) preceded by an anteroom (*procoeton*), both with simple linear decoration on the walls and vault. The tiny pillared court by which they are preceded for the provision of light and air has an almost claustral flavour (PL. XXVIII, *fig. 51*).

Those who have time at their disposal, should here visit two little houses flanking the " Casa dell'Alcova ,,.

HOUSE (*Insula IV, n. 5–6–7*). – It is a modest habitation, perhaps inhabited by a family of shopkeepers or artisans. The front part was used for the exercise of the business and the more private, withdrawn rear portion formed the living quarters. On one side of the *fauces* is a simple workroom (*n. 5*) and on the other a shop (*n. 7*). Behind the shop, in the covered *atrium*, there is a typical installation of podia and tanks for the washing of clothes. At the end of the *atrium*, there is a larger room (the *triclinium*) and an *apotheca*; behind these, arranged around another Tuscan *atrium* with an *impluvium* tank, are the few other ground–floor rooms. The two rooms at the end, with the original barrel–vaulting, good *opus signinum* pavements with sections in marble *opus sectile* and lit by circular windows, still preserve the remains of a nobler, more antique decoration in the I style in the fine stucco cornice with dentils and in the mouldings of the lunette of the vault.

HOUSE (*Insula IV, n. 8–9*). – This house has two entrances, one for the ground floor and a smaller one (*n. 9*) for the upper floor, which in this case also has a gallery overhanging the street pavement; between the two entrances is a *podium*. The house, with a long, narrow ground–plan, unfolds itself longitudinally beyond all traditional measure, without an *atrium* in the centre but with a simple light–well at the end. The *fauces* which lie to one side are prolonged across the whole house to the rear and the different rooms open upon them as upon the corridor of a modern flat. The last spacious room at the back has a beautiful motif in the IV style painted on the upper part of the wall, of draped curtains disclosing an architectural view.

On the left side–walk, at n. 13, opens the entrance to the interesting.

CASA A GRATICCIO (*OPUS CRATICIUM*) (*Insula III, n. 13–14–15*). – Together with various Samnite houses of a patrician character, Herculaneum has also given us in this humble habitation an admirably preserved example of the popular economic type of dwelling, constructed with a humbler technique and poorer materials than those usually adopted; it is constructed in *opus craticium,* with the skeleton of the walls in wood, or simply of cane–trellising, a system recorded by Vitruvius, who justifies it only for reasons of celerity or where the soil is unsuitable for heavy constructions and points out that it has the grave drawback of being both inflammable and susceptible to the damp of the subsoil. There are abundant examples of this technique at Pompeii towards the end in dwellings of a commercial character, where it was used for the subordinate parts of a house, such as galleries or superstructures but this Herculanean abode is the first organic and complete example of an entire edifice constructed in such a way on the ground and first floors. The whole mural skeleton of the house, with the exception of the outer walls and the few remaining parts of a pre–existing structure, is composed of brick pilasters and wooden frames filled with *opus incertum* cemented with abundant lime–mortar, the whole then being covered by the customary stratum of stucco and painted rough–cast (*tectorium*).

This house is also the clearest example in Pompeian and Herculanean building of a house let out to various families who have in common only the light of the inner courtyard and the water from the well, as is to be seen from the plan and distribution of the rooms and the division of these into two apartments, the one accessible from the *fauces* of the ground floor (*n. 14*), the other from the door and stairs at *n. 13*.

Overlooking the road, there is a little portico and a gallery with a small covered room on it (PL. XI, *fig. 20*). The low, wide *fauces* (the ceiling beams reproduce exactly the original beams found in a carbonized state) lead into a small courtyard instead of the usual *atrium*, closed all round by a high podium. Over this look out the different rooms, with the wide horizontal windows of the ground floor and the narrow vertical one with low sills of the upper storey. We have here in germ the courtyard of a modern block of flats of several storeys let out to a number of families. (PL. XII, *fig. 21*). One of the ground floor rooms, probably used as a work–room, communicates with the shop that opens upon the street: an artisan's house and workshop (PL., XII, *fig. 22*). The upper floor is reached by a staircase which retains several of its original steps. Here, a narrow *cubiculum* vivacioulsy painted in red and another room but little larger both preserve their ancient furniture: the wooden bedsteads, against the walls, a cupboard with the few remaining utensils, a few other objects and statuettes of the *Lares* and of divinities, and a marble table: the surroundings of humble folk, still humanly alive.

The other apartment (*n. 13*), separated by a central corridor, also had to resolve for itself with modest expedients the problems of lack of space and inadeguate lighting; the only light and airy room was that opening upon the open gallery, and here there were found, together with a *triclinium* couch, the little front of a wooden shrine and a head also roughly carved in wood, both belonging to the domestic *lararium*.

At the corner of the cardo and the decumanus is the:

CASA DEL TRAMEZZO DI LEGNO (*Insula III, n. 11–12*). – This offers, with its front preserved up to the second storey, and the portal, windows and small lights which break it at various heights, one of the completest examples of a private house façade at either Pompeii or Herculaneum. Above the ovuled cornice, there is an open gallery supported by beams of carbonized wood belonging to a later superstructure, of the last years of the city (PL. XIII, *fig. 13*). The clearly patrician house originally extended across the entire *insula*; later, some of the rooms overlooking the *decumanus* and the *III cardo* were detached and made to serve more humbly as shops and artisan's homes. Here, too, the construction of a second floor above the *atrium* roof, with a separate entrance at *n. 10*, marks the gradual passage here and elsewhere at Herculaneum from the noble *domus* of a single family the house where several families dwelt together with various common rights and uses which the law of private right would gradually regulate.

The *fauces* open upon one of the most grandiose atria known to us, even at Pompeii, with a compluviate roof (the dog's head spouts are some of them original) of the Tuscan type. The *impluvium* tank has a double lining, in *opus signinum* and in marble, having been revetted first during the Republican era and later during the Claudian or Neronian period. The wall decoration is preserved up to the top of the first floor. On the right of the *fauces* is an elegant cubicle with a fine mosaic pavement with a geometrical design and a table of " fior di pesco ,, marble, supported by a figure of the Phrygian god Atthis, from the upper floor; on the left side of the *atrium* there are two other *cubicula* with the frames of wooden beds and an *exedra* (PL. XV, *fig. 25*).

But the element so singular and exceptional as to have given its name to the house is the wooden partition with three double-leaved doors, of which the central one is lacking; it has been possible to reconstruct this *in situ*, where it formerly closed the wide opening of the *tablinum*, so that what had once been a room of passage became an airy, sheltered reception room suitable for the siesta. Its wooden leaves, extricated from the hardened mud, swing once more upon their ancient hinges and the bronze lamp–supports, in the form of a ship's stern ornaments, are fixed once more in the upright posts (PL. XIV, *fig. 24*; PL. XVI, *fig. 27*). The glass cases in the *atrium* and in the *tablinum* contain objects found in the house; especially to be noted are the remains of dried vegetables (beans).

Behind the *tablinum* there is a small and charming garden, surrounded by a little pilastered portico with cubicles and rooms for repose around it. The central room on the west side served as the *triclinium*; it was brought to light in the old excavations and the decoration is very deteriorared, as in the other rooms surrounding it. On the south wall there is painted a pleasing garden view with trellising, bushes, a marble urn and ducks feeding.

We have here reached the decumanus inferior; on its front towards west, opens a series of shops and dwellings :

SHOPS. – The shops and more modest lodgings to the west, north and south of the above stately dwelling must also have belonged to the same proprietor, either let out by him or managed for him by freedmen and slaves. There was a little communicating door between the small garden portico and the backshop of the large shop on the corner of the *decumanus* (*n. 6*) with its adjoining premises; from the *atrium* of the house there were two exits with steps leading to the ground floor of the great shop which had two entrances on the same *decumanus* (*n. 8–9*). The shop on the north west corner, on the other hand, lacks any direct communication with the inside of the house (*n. 10*); it has a very low ceiling and in it was found a wooden press with a central screw for pressing clothes, which for its singular state of preservation constitutes a true and precious *unicum* in ancient technology. It was undoubtedly the shop of a clothes–mercant, a *lanarius*. The upper floor was reached from the shop by a small staircase (PL. XV, *fig. 26*).

Finally, the entrance at *n. 12*, with its door–keeper's cubby-hole placed in mid–air upon rafters (this immediately reminds us of similar arrangements still to be seen in the popular quarters of Naples), led by means of a high, steep staircase, to the separate apartments of the first and second floors; these lay partly along the main front of the house, partly along the south wing of the *atrium*.

He, who likes to make a complete visit of the excavations, may, here, reach on the cardo III, the

CASA DELLO SCHELETRO (*Insula III, n. 3*). – This house was so–named from a skeleton found during the excavations of 1831 in one of the rooms on the upper floor. It was only partly disinterred in 1830–31, the work being completed in 1927–28. It is not a large house, and almost all the many rooms are somewhat small, but they display distinction wealth in their distribution and decoration. Since, owing to lack of space, there was neither garden nor portico to air the internal rooms, the architect designed tiny courtyards and light–wells, one of them being decorated as a shrine and a *nymphaeum* in communication with the ground–floor reception rooms. Notable remains of the upper storey came to light in the 1830–31 excavations; they were inadequately protected and are now almost entirely in ruins. It is probable that the whole south wing, connected with the *atrium* by a single corridor, was a later addition to the primitive nucleus.

The *atrium*, without the *impluvium* tank, is of the rarer testudinate type, frequently found at Herculaneum; that is, it was entirely roofed over, with an outward sloping roof, with the consequent draining–off of the rainwater in that direction. In the left wing there is a spacious *triclinium* opening upon a charming *nymphaeum*, with twin tanks with marblefaced borders and the back wall treated architecturally, with imitation bossed masonry on the lower portion and a mosaic frieze on the upper. The panels, framed with bands of shells and azure glasspaste, are faced with rough–cast, as in the *nymphaea* of Italian Cinquecento villas. The frieze in glasspaste, with an azure ground and copper–green and bright red panels, also bordered by shells, was originally adorned with subjects suggested by landscape paintings; only three panels remain, the rest having been destroyed by the wretched tunnelling.

Another very elegant room is that with the apse behind the *tablinum*, at the end of the *atrium*. In the little courtyard which aired and illuminated this room there is a *nymphaeum* whose principal adornment is the precious little shrine on a high *podium* reveted with glass–paste in a geometric design with ornamental motifs: in the centre of the niche, the visage of a fermale divinity looks out from a tuft of acanthus leaves. A garden painting completes the wall–decoration. The courtyard was protected at the top by an iron grille, a necessary precaution owing to the contiguity of neighbouring roofs and the facility of the drop down into the court (PL. XVI, *fig. 28*). In the wing to the south of the *atrium* is to be noted the group of rooms at the end, easily recognizable as a small apartment distinct from the rest of the house; the last of these rooms is a still, tranquil *cubiculum* with a vaulted ceiling, black walls, and a pavement in white mosaic, which receives its air from a narrow light–well inserted in the interstice between two walls.

INSULA VI

HOUSE WITH TWO COURTYARDS. – In the high part of the *cardo III* where at present ends the disinterment of the street, after the entrance n. I of the *Thermae*, there has recently been uncovered a dwelling (without number). It preserves a beautiful façade in *opus reticulatum* with portal and architrave in tufa and a long brick frame. Above it open the windows of the upper rooms, which were reached by means of a doorway opening on the street. The house has a narrow and lengthened plan with development of the upper floors disclosed by the height of the walls and the holes left by the beams). Inside, two *atria*, the first tetrastylon, the second of tuscanic type with the *impluvium* closed by a parapet and a beautiful *puteal* on the edge of the well. Close to the entrance, are the kitchen and the oven. But the living rooms develope around the little *atrium*: on the north, a room elegantly painted in the richest scheme of the IV style (in the southern wall two niches of *lararia*); on the east opens a wide tricliniar hall, as the only preserved picture representing two mullets and two pears bears wittness. Staircases led to the rooms of the first and second floor.

THE THERMAE
(see plan, fig. 4)

The Thermae occupy a large part of *Insula VI* and, lying as they do between the greater and lesser *decumani*, they are in immediate contact with the central quarters of the city. Though smaller than the Pompeian Baths, with less refined, less perfected heating apparatus, etc., they show the same distribution of the various localities and the same rigorius division of the two sections of the men's and women's baths, whilst at the same time they have a more rational, organic plan due to the homogeneity of their construction which was completed during a single period and underwent no substantial modifications.

They were probably erected during the early Augustan period (30–10 B. C.); the decoration is later, of the time of either Claudius or Nero. During the 1860–75 excavations, only the *palaestra* and the shops on the western side were disinterred; the recent explorations have completed the work and the *Thermae* are thus the first public edifice of Herculaneum to have reappeared in its entirety whilst excavations are still in course in the Palaestra and in the suburban Baths.

There are four a distinct entrances one on the *III cardo* (*n. 1*), the real main entrance to the men's Baths, and three on the *IV cardo*, that is, one at *n. 7* which leads to the *palaestra* and across that to the mens' bath, one at *n. 8* leading exclusively to the women's section, and another at *n. 10*, a service door leading to the *praefurnium* (boiler–furnace), and to other parts of the water–supply plant.

MEN's THERMAE (*III cardo, n. 1*). – A corridor flanked by a half–destroyed latrine, and by a tiny rectangular room with a small square window, probably that of the door–keeper of the men's section, leads in one direction to the portico of the *palaestra* which also served as a rest room where the clients of the Baths awaited their turn, and in the other, through a little doorway to the dressing room (*apodyterium*) (PL. XVII, *fig. 30*).

This latter is a large room, the best preserved in the men's section, with a simple red dado, a strigilated stucco vault and a pavement in *opus segmentatum* in black, grey and white marble, slightly convex in order to facilitate the washing thereof. Around three sides of the room runs the plain *podium* for the seats, and the shelves with separate recesses for clothes and bath linen. In an apse on the end wall there is a beautiful basin (*labrum*) of *cipollino* marble and another basin in the corner, both used for the ablution of hands and feet before entering the *frigidarium* or the *tepidarium*. A large round window in the upper part of the south wall was sufficient to light the room, similar to those to be seen in other parts of the men's and women's baths. Two glass cases in the centre of the room contain the remains of the two skeleton found under the mud—flow on this spot, the first victims discovered in the area of the new excavations; they were probably the custodians of the Thermae who had descended from the upper floor in order to take vain refuge under the robust vault of the *tepidarium*, when they were submerged under the tide of mud.

The small square room leads to the round tank of the *frigidarium* painted marine blue, with red walls broken by four deep niches and a domed ceiling (with a skylight) upon which is painted a fishpond on a bluish ground: fat eels mullet and *aguglie* and a gigantic polype grasping a muraena. The vault teflected in the azure waters of the bath must have created rhe illusion of an aquarium and the bathers must have felt themselves to be completely immersed in a marine atmosphere of sky and water.

The great *tepidarium* with the hollow floor, now largely caved in, has the same system of *podia* and shelves around it as the *apodyterium*. The mosaic pavement of somewhat coarse workmanship has a representation of a galloping Triton with a helm and a basked of fruit surrounded by four dolphins (the same subject as that in the women's *apodyterium*). The *calidarium* in arranged as is usual in Roman *calidaria*: there is the bath for immersion at one end of the room and the *podium* for the cold water *labrum* at the other end in a shell—shaped apse. The fallen vault gives us a clear view of the smoke-vents built behind the vault and of the hot—air pipes laid in the thickness of the walls.

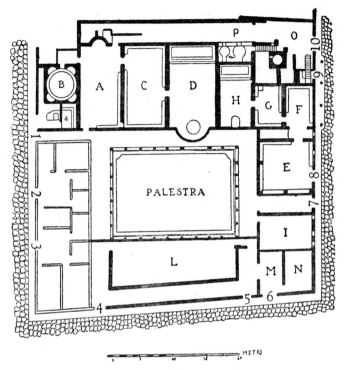

FIG. 4 — GROUND—PLAN OF THE THERMAE

I – Entrance of the men's baths	F – Apodyterium of the women's baths
a – Latrine	G – Tepidarium of the women's baths
A – Apodyterium of the men's baths	H – Calidarium of the women's baths
B – Frigidarium of the men's baths	I – Apodyterium of the palaestra
C – Tepidarium of the men's baths	L – Sphaeristerium (?)
D – Calidarium of the men's baths	9 – Cella ostiaria
7 – Entrance to the palaestra	10 – Entrance to the praefurnium
8 – Entrance to the women's baths	O – Well and water–tower
E – Vestibule of the women's baths	P – Praefurnium

Retracing our steps we reach the courtyard of the *palaestra*, an essential element in mens' baths, surrounded here as in the Stabian and Forum Thermae at Pompeii by a portico along three of its sides, with columns and pilasters in brick–work faced with stucco, but without any basin. The fragment of decoration which remains in the north–east corner is in the typical linear architectural manner of the pompeian IV style (PL. XVII, *fig. 29*).

The use of the rectangular space connected with the *palaestra* with two separate entrances along the *decumanus* (*n. 4–5*) and which also communicates with the corner shop is unknown: it was probably a covered playground with a penthouse roof, perhaps a *spheristerium* where the ball–game (*pila*) was played.

The *palaestra* was reached from the other great entrance on the *IV cardo* (*n. 7*) and beside the fauces there were two rooms for the use of the *palaestra* players (*districtarium*).

WOMEN'S BATHS. – As in the Pompeian Baths, the section reserved to women was smaller, less well decorated and less complete than the men's section (here the *frigidarium* bath is entirely lacking but to make up for this the different parts are better preserved and there is an atmosphere of greater and richer intimacy. The entrance is, as we have said, at *n. 8* on the *IV cardo*.

The first large square room (*Plan, fig. 4–E*), decorated with a simple red dado and with a continuous podium all round, where the clients waited their turn often for a long time, leads, through another tiny rectangular vestibule where the bath linen was probably distributed, to the small charming *apodyterium* with the usual shelf with recesses running around it and a strigilated stucco vault; the mosaic pavement, executed with an impressionistic technique, is similar to that in the *tepidarium* in the men's baths: a large Triton in the centre surrounded by dolphins, polyps and eels. The *tepidarium*, smaller than the preceding room, has the usual shelf divided into separate recesses for clothes and bath linen and a finer mosaic pavement with the geometrical meander motif (PL. XVIII, *fig. 31*). The *calidarium* with the hollow floor and the smoke and heat vents placed in the thickness of the walls, as in the men's section, presents us with a more complete view of the typical arrangements of the *calidaria* of the I century of the Empire: there is the large marble bath for the hot bath and, opposite to it, the circular *podium* for a bronze or marble *labrum* for the cold or tepid water ablutions (the basin has been carried away from here also); along the walls, there are two elegant marble benches for the rest between the *sudatio* and the bath (PL. XVIII, *fig. 32*).

Leaving the women's Baths and following the street–pavement, we reach (after passing *n. 2*, a small den under the stairs leading to the upper terraces of the edifice) the last entrance to the north, *n. 10*, that of the service quarters which run along behind the men's and women's sections in the form of one wide corridor. The vestibule wall still bears the incrustation of smoke and soot that was diffused when the *praefurnium* was lit or stoked. On the left on entering, there is a straight staircase, partly in wood and partly in masonry which led to the attics and terraces. Further ahead, there is the deep circular well whence the water was raised by means of a chain pump to the reservoirs; nearby there is the little staircase used in the inspection of the boilers and, finally, the furnace (*praefurnium*) for each of the two boilers which fed the men's and women's baths respectively. The boilers were carried away during the Bourbon excavations but there remains the heavy iron door of the *praefurnium* used to heat the water for the men's baths, and near it lies the great iron poker for raking the embers and cinders, a sign that the bath functioned up to the last moment before the eruption. At the end of the great service corridor, a small door opened into the *apodyterium* of the men's section, whilst a wooden staircase led to the living quarters on the upper floor, occupied by the personnel of the Baths.

Near to the Baths, but independent of them, there are to be noted various rustic quarters opening upon the *III cardo* at *n. 2–3*, at a lower level than the *palaestra*; they were shops and humble habitations.

On the cardo IV, close to the Thermae, opens the entrance to a dwelling not yet entirely disinterred.

HOUSE OF THE BLACK HALL (*n. 11*). – After the entrance of the *praefurnium* of the Thermae, following the raised and porticoed side–walk, one passes through a secondary entrance (the main entrance still buried must open on the *decumanus*), in to the courtyard of a patrician dwelling, surrounded by an elegant columned portico. In the southern side thereof open two beautiful *cubicula*; the little vaults preserve all the ornamental motives plainly painted; in the western side opens a large black hall, with the walls divided in three painted rectangulars like mirrors, flanked by pillars and chandeleers of lively colours.

The ceiling too, with a wide skylight in the centre, recomposed from various fragments, is on a black ground. Against the wall is placed a wooden shrine in the usual form of a little temple, with wooden columns and little marble capitals, which preserved the little statues of a Lararium. At present, the remaining parts of the dwelling are shill hidden under the mound of the lava flow.

Ret us return to the lower decumanus to visit the series of the beautiful houses of the insula V on the cardo IV:

SAMNITE HOUSE (*Insula V, n. 1-2*). – This house preserves more than any other the architecture and structure of the Samnite type of habitation at Herculaneum, notwithstanding the modifications and mutilations it underwent. It is preceded by a stretch of finer street–paving; two podia fiank the entrance. The beautiful portal has the jambs in *opus quadratum*, surmounted by Corinthian capitals. The open gallery that overhangs the porch and runs along the whole façade is due as in the case of the neighbouring " Casa del tramezzo di legno ,, , to a later extension of the upper storey, when (by means of the adjoining entrance, *n. 2*, and steep wooden stairs) the rooms above the main doorway were detached from the rest of the house, forming a tiny apartment to let (PL. XXII, *fig. 39*).

In the interior, the *fauces* retain their typical decoration in the I style, that is, an imitation of polychrome marble bossed works (the only well–preserved example found so far at Herculanum). They lead into the most beautiful atrium (a unique example in domestic architecture), with a charming covered gallery above, with little Ionic columns closed by a perforated parapet or *pluteus*, faced with fine stucco, the architectural motive of the loggias of Hellenistic porticoes. Here, in the *atrium* of this small Herculanean house, we have in embryo the forms and structures which the Italian Renaissance will later spread abroad in the courts of palaces and villas. At present the intercolumnar spaces are open only on the east side, in such a way as abundantly to light and air the *atrium*; originally, that is, before the first floor rooms overlooking the street were let out, there must have been some windows along the west and north wings (PL. XXII, *fig. 40*).

The house, deprived of the garden that must once have belonged to it, has few rooms on the ground floor but all are decorated with a certain distinction. A cubicle to the right of the *fauces* is delicately decorated in pale sea–green monochrome, with architectural details shadowed in and a picture with the *Rape of Europa* in the centre. A larger room of the left has walls with a red ground and rough *graffiti*. The *tablinum* was adorned with a pavement in *opus signinum* with tessellated work, and communicates with another well–decorated room.

An inner room led to the apartments of the south wing of the gallery.

Amongst the objects found during the excavations and now exhibited in the *atrium* there are: a mutilated statuette of *Venus* putting on her sandal, several fragments of wooden feet from table–legs carved in the form of a dog running, and among the comestibles, a basin full of small cakes.

CASA DEL TELAIO (*Insula V, n. 3–4*). – This house is in complete contrast with the distinguished Samnite house and was probably the house and workshop of artisans, possibly cloth–makers and merchants (*textores*). The entrance, *n. 5*, with a long, narrow *fauces*, leads to the extremely simple living quarters on the ground floor and to the little internal court closed by a portico with brick columns (along one of its sides were gathered the scanty remains of carbonized wood and several weights from a loom). The next entrance, *n. 4*, leads to what was probably the real and true factory and workroom, and perhaps the storeroom and shop as well. The whole of the front part of the edifice was covered by one great roof, whose eaves far overhung the pavement; the large locality on the left of the entrance originally had an uninterrupted series of loop–holes under the roof, later filled in.

CASA DEL MOBILIO CARBONIZZATO (*Insula V, n. 5*). – This house, like the " Casa dello scheletro ,, , the " Casa dell'erma di bronzo ,, and the " Casa dell'atrio corintio ,, , belongs to that type of small but distinguished dwelling (*parva sed apta*) of the middle classes of Herculaneum which, without commercial lucre or brazen–faced shop–keeping, succeeded in defending the integrity of the old patriarchial abode from the avid overbearingness of the rich and the invasion of the new–rich. The doorway still of ample proportions, the height of the *fauces,* the architectural scheme of the little *atrium* where on a lesser scale there is the same disposition as on the upper floor, open along one side and closed on the other, that we have seen in so harmonious and powerful a guise in the neighbouring " Samnite House ,, (s. p. 40), and, finally, the general arrangement in the traditional manner of the rooms around the *atrium* and the little back courtyard are all characteristic of a house pre-Roman in date, plan and structure. The wall–decorations were renewed, however, and all belong to the same period (Claudian) and come from the same hand; though of no particular interest artistically, they give a tone of fresh and vibrating gaiety to the interior. The view from the *fauces,* with the little temple–shrine on the end wall of the courtyard, forms a delicious perspective intentionally planned by the owner (PL. XXI, *figs. 37–38*).

On the right of the *fauces* there is the principal room, the *triclinium*, with beautiful, sumptuous decoration in the IV style and a pavement in coloured marble tiles. There are little pictures on the walls: one with a cock bending with open beak before a bunch of cherries, and a still–life, with mushrooms (?), dates, figs and walnuts (?). On the left of the *fauces* there is in alcove with an anteroom; they originally formed a single room before being divided by a light partition, as is clearly to be seen from the pavement design. At the end of the *atrium* are the small elegant *tablinum* (to be noted the flying and floating female figures above the niches) and a little room for the siesta and to work in (*diaeta*), with a large window looking upon the courtyard and a tiny painting of *Pan* approaching a sleeping nymph on one of the walls.

A pleasant inside room, more intimate and withdrawn, opens with a triple window upon the little court: against one of the walls there is a wooden *triclinium* couch in the form of a divan, with the side and head veneered, and beside it a small wooden table with glass and terracotta vases upon it. The little court, closed all round by a parapet and paved in *opus signinum*, with a circular flower–bed left open in the centre and several other openings for bushes, was chiefly designed to collect and conduct away the rainwater to the cistern. The charming *Lararium* which decorates this humble court, the airy windows that look out upon it and the bushes which still grow there, all give it an unspeakable grace, an air of intimate, serene family life.

CASA DEL MOSAICO DI NETTUNO E DI ANFITRITE (*Insula V, n. 6–7*). – The outside wall of the upper open gallery was overthrown either by the earthquake accompanying the eruption or by the onslaught of the lava flow and the interior of the rooms is to be seen from the street, as if rudely unveiled in all their intimacy. A large shop flanks the entrance on the ground floor and on the upper floor there are the living quarters overlooking the street; their partition walls are still well decorated. There is a *cubiculum* amongst them with a wooden bedstead, a candelabrum and a marble monopod (*trapeza*) (PL. XIX, *fig. 33*).

The shop, amongst the hundreds and hundreds which have been found at Pompeii, is the most miracolously preserved, best fusnished shop of antiquity. On the great counter near the entrance still lie the shop–fittings and the goods of the last day and last hours of business and inside, on shelves, there are the wine amphorae, in upright and lying positions according to their need, which were either emptied or sold in the shop. Behind the counter is a sort of wooden partition with a close grating that has a distinct flavour of a convent grille. In the corners are the fireplace and the sink (PL. XIX, *fig. 34*).

We know nothing of the proprietor of this well–supplied shop but, to judge from the interior of the house, the grandiose *atrium*, the sumptuousness of several rooms and the small bronzes and painted marble panels by neo–Attic artists found near the *lararium*, the taste and spirit of this unknown citizen of Herculaneum must not have been too dissimilar to that of the wealthy merchants of the Renaissance, who loved to take refuge from the wool–merchant's selling–counter in a beautiful house rich in works of art.

The little internal courtyard is particularly beautiful, with the vivacious chromatic effect of the precious mosaic revetment of the walls, thus adorned in the grand patrician manner by the fortunate owner as if in compensation for the lack of a portico, of a garden, of a wide view of sea and sky. In the open, surrounded by the sparkling mosaic walls, is the low *triclinium* table, raised but little above the level of the ground. The end walls is turned into a *nymphaeum* with a central rounded niche flanked by two smaller rectangular ones, the whole façade being faced by glass–paste mosaic, admirably preserved. At the sides of the niches there are represented earthenware jugs (*canthari*) from which spring long sprays of vine leaves; above, on a blue ground, beneath rich festoons of fruit and foliage, there is a hunting scene with hounds and fleeing deer. The backs and borders of the niches are adorned with shells and madreporic concretions, as they will be later on in the fountains of Quattrocento and Cinquecento gardens and villas. The luxurious whole is surmounted by theatrical masks and a superb head of a Silenus with traces of vivid polychromy, like *acroteria*; above rises the end wall of the court (PL. XX, *fig. 35*).

On the other wall, facing the entrance to the house, in a frame surmounted by a conch, there is a representation in a mosaic panel of a mythological subject, *Neptune and Amphitrite*. Because of its vegetable and animalistic motifs and the daring impressionistic treatment, this Herculanean mosaic is one of the most eloquent testimonies to the continuity of the art of mosaic wall revetemnt from the Alexandrian and Roman periods to the Christian and Byzantine era.

In the room preceding the courtyard with the nympheum, there is a small and attractive bronze herma of *Hercules* (in a glass case in the centre); a beautiful statuette of Jupiter was found in the *atrium* (PL. XX, *fig. 36*).

Preceded by a front in which open little windows closed by grills, we reach beyond the entrance to the.

CASA DEL BEL CORTILE (*Insula V, n. 8*). – It is a dwelling which, though of small proportions, is particularly interesting for the novelty of its plan. Instead of the usual *fauces* and *vestibulum*, one enters a low wide rectangular room, which leads to other rooms, partly rustic (on the right), partly decorated (on the left). Among the latter, there are a little kitchen and a tricliniar hall, lighted by the courtyard. The raised courtyard preserves a fine mosaic pavement; it has no *impluvium*, but an adequate inclination of the floor lets the rain water flow in to a gutter and a well.

As in the courtyard of the houses of the Italian Middle–Age, it developes a flight of steps in masonry and a gallery with a parapet soberly painted; in the understaircase, on the ground wall there is the painting of leafy vine–branch, giving the impression of a garden trellis in the open air.

In the upper floor one may recognize some rooms looking on the street from the usual gallery. The great hall of the ground floor, on the south of the courtyard, is the only room remaining of a larger dwelling anterior to 62 A. D., once connected with the nearby House of the Bicentenario (see 45 page).

The *cardo* developes deeply embanked between two high sidewalks; at its crossing with the decumanus, there is a pillar (cut off at 1/3 of its height), with painted inscriptions; one of them, preserving rules of street police, is probably an ordnance of the *aediles*; on one side there is an *ara compitalis* with serpents (*agathodaimon*) flanking it; in front of it, leaning partly at the side–walk of the *decumanus*, there is a public fountain with two water–spouts; it is at present hidden under the platform on which the modern houses of Resína are still standing. The fountain preserves on a side a rough representation of Venus bathing on the other a mask of Gorgon.

We have here reached the decumanus maximus (see p. 48):

SHOP (*Ins. V, n. 10*) (with a secondary entrance on the *cardo*, at n. 9). Here are to be seen the big pots set in the ground, which preserved cereals and dry vegetables. For the same purpose was also used the little porch of the side–walk on the western side, (a lot of cereals indeed was found there). The shop belonged to the following dwelling, as it is clearly shown by a little door, through which the two dwellings were connected.

House (*Insula V, n. 11–12*). – This was a noble–dwelling, originally vaster once it was connected with the nearby house of the Bicentenario through a passage, afterwards walled in.

In the walls of the *atrium* are to be seen the empty spaces left by the main beams once supporting the planking of the compluviate roof. Traces here and there of rough modifications show that, in the last years, the house had assumed a more mercantile character.

Noble, however, appears the decoration of the *tablinum*, with its sectile pavement (not too unlike that of the *tablinum* in the house of the Bicentenario), and the walls divided in to yellow rectangulars like mirrors. On the ground wall a panel with Apollo playing the zithern and crowned with laurel, a Nymph, and on one side, an Cupid supporting the god's heavy quiver.

The room *n. 12*, transformed into a shop, preserves, leaning against the wall, a simple wooden cupboard, with horizontal boards.

Shop with dwelling (*Insula V, n. 13–14*). – Though at present independent, originally it belonged to the house of the Bicentenario. The shop, without the installment of a counter and furniture of *amphorae* for the storing of eatables, more probably is to be considered an artisan's shop. Near by, there was the staircase to ascend to the dwelling quarter.

House of the Bicentenario (*Insula V, n. 15–16*). – The house owes its name to the fact that its disinterment began in the year 1938 just two hundred years after the beginning of the excavations of Herculaneum (1738). The entrance to this house, the noblest and richest private building of the *insula V*, opens along the *decumanus maximus*, among a series of shops and humble dwellings.

The house, however, underwent, in the last years of the life of the city, the same rough transformations we have already noted in other private buildings. The whole ground floor still preserves the traditional plan of a Roman house. A *vestibulum* and the *fauces* lead to the wide square atrium with compluviate roof (the main beams have been situated in their original place again); the beautiful pavement in mosaic with simple white tesserae on the black ground preserves around the marble *impluvium*, a band with the motiv of tresses; the walls are painted a beautiful red–porphyry.

In the back ground of the *atrium*, on the sides of the *tablinum*, open the two *alae*: the one on the right, closed by a wooden gate had to preserve the shrine of the *Lares*, or, perhaps, as the family was a patrician one, the shrine for the worship of the *imagines maiorum*. The *tablinum* preserves a rich, sparkling marble pavement, like a polycrom carpet, and, on the walls, paintings, medaillons, and a frieze; in the panels are represented the myths of *Daedalus* and *Pasifae* and of *Venus* and *Mars;* in the medaillons are busts of *Satyrs, Silens* and *Maenades.* On the upper part of the wall, runs a frieze with Eroten. From the *tablinum*, we reach the little portico with the garden and the rustic rooms of the ground–floor.

Christian oratory. – The dwelling quarters occupying the upper floor of the portico present themselves very humbly indeed; in the last years of the city they had no longer been reserved to the *familia* of servants, but, instead, when the ground floor, deprived of its fittings, was abandoned by the ancient rich proprietors, they became the actual rented lodgings of some modest family of artisans or merchants. In a room of this quarter on the wall facing the entrance is to be noted a symbol in shape of a cross inserted in to a stuccoed panel; originally there was a big wooden Cross inserted and nailed in to the socket; besides as would appear from the presence of iron–hooks on the sides of the panel, the Cross was preserved by wooden wickets supported by a frame, just as a holy symbol.

Under the panel with the Cross was found (and is at present on the spot), a low wooden cupboard with a step on the front, in the shape of a little *ara* or wooden shrine with a foot–stool. Doubtelessly the religious importance of the symbol of the Cross and of the wooden furniture is interesting; the interpretation given at the moment of the discovery that it would be a private Christian oratory is at present strengthened by the most widespread and authoritative assents, notwithstanding lively polemics and discussions. Thanks to this discovery, the Christian cult of the Cross, officially established after Constantin's edict and till now documented by few monuments as belonging to the II and III century, would date back to the time anterior to the 79 A. D., i. e. to the earliest time of Apostolic Preaching. The introduction of this cult to Herculaneum would be attributed to St. Paul's preaching. This humble room of the House of the Bicentenario preserves, therefore, one of the most precious testimonies of the oldest history of the Church.

Let us now return to the street, passing through the atrium, and glance from below at the rooms of the quarters situated on the front of the street, reached by the staircase that developed in the room, *n. 16*; the traces of the decoration, and the paintings of a *Lararium* show that this dwelling, independent from the remaining part, was inhabited, at the moment of the eruption, by the last important lodger of the whole dwelling. Surely he was or a survivor of the ancient patrician family, or, more probably, a *procurator* or manager of the proprietors, who, after the earthquake of 62 A. D., prefered to live in another house in the city, or in the suburb.

SHOP WITH BACK-SHOP AND DWELLING (*Insula V, n. 17–18*). – This shop without counter, but with the installment of a little kitchen, back-shop almost elegantly decorated and with confortable dwelling quarters on the upper floor, seems more suitable to an artisan's exigencies than to a Mecenate's.

Ingenious the utilisation of the space: in the understaircase there is a cupboard, and upon it a loft for the storage of household goods. On the upper floor (seen from the back-shop), one sees a wooden shrine in the form of a little temple with fronton and columns. Near it, the excavations have brought to light a beautiful panel representing a group of playing Eroten; this panel is executed according to the unusual technique of the panel enclosed in strong wooden frames; they were made in the shops and afterwards inserted in the decoration of the walls.

SHOPS (*Insula V, n. 19–20*). – N. 19 and 20 are two connected shops with backshop; as they have been intersected by the underground galleries, at present they preserve neithel decoration, nor furniture; in one of them there is the usuar installment of the kitchen and latrine.

SHOP WITH DWELLING ON THE CORNER OF THE STREET (*Insula V, n. 21–22*). – Similarly to the shops situated at the cross-roads, also this, notwithstanding the considerable transformations which it underwent, appears to us wider than the others. The counter is placed against one of the walls; on the background opens a room reserved to the clients, and a little *cubiculum* for the manager of for the guardian.

The dwelling quarter of the upper floor (which is reached by the entrance at n. 22) is comfortable and preserves a plain decoration; one of the rooms, divided from the others by a framework and used as bedroom, was lighted by a square window, which still preserves a part of its wooden folding-doors.

The excavations of these last five years, bringing to light a part of the *decumanus maximus*, have prepared the way for the explanation of the problem concerning the discovery of the Forum, center of the religious and civil life of the city. At present, one may reach the *decumanus maximus* by two streets, the *cardines* IV and V, both entirely uncovered in their southern part.

The *decumanus maximus* is very large compared with the others streets of Herculaneum (it measures more than 12 metres); on the northern and southern sides it presents side-walks of 3 or 4 mt. in width; but only the northern side-walk was with porches, and not the other, as the plans of the ancient excavations erronously show. In the little square, from which begins the *decumanus*, there is a public Fountain with the representation of *Hercules*. That, however, this wide street was not used for cars but only for pedestrians, is shown by two facts: firstly, it is not paved with blocks of Vesuvian or calcarious stone; secondly, two travertin piliars along the edge of the *cardo V* and a high step along that of the *cardo IV* mark the limit of the cart-road.

Besides, the low side-walks and the brick gutters, flanking the street, clearly prove that this central street, starting from the fountain of Hercules towards west, was only reserved to pedestrians. We note the same thing at Pompeii, where the roads opening on the civil Forum are barred by street-posts and high stone steps. It is, jhowever, natural to suppose that this street with many shops and work shops of artisans with public buildings as the Basilica, was placed in the area of the Forum.

The next excavations will show whether this street widened out into a square, or had, on its western end, the biggest temple of the city, as it is shown in La Vega's city plan.

At the cross-roads of the decumanus maximus with the cardo V opens, on the eastern front of the street, the entrance to an imposing hall, that, together with a series of shops and dwellings, belongs to the insula orientalis II (see p. 53). Let us visit for the present the houses of the western front of the street:

CASA DELL'ATRIO CORINTIO (*Insula V, n. 30*). – This house is small, with few rooms on the ground floor, but it is in good taste, and must have belonged to people of the leisured middle classes of Herculaneum. Externally, it is preceded by a little portico prolonged down to the *decumanus*, and by a stretch of better pavement adorned with marble. Internally, the *fauces* with three steps lead to a graceful polystyle *atrium* with six tufa columns (three on either side) faced with red and white stucco, disposed around the *impluvium* tank crossed by the low channels of a cruciform fountain (PL. XXIV, *fig. 43*). In a room to the right of the *fauces* there is a mosaic pavement with a fine geometric design in which recurs a formalized version of the sacred double–edged axe (*labrys*). In a glass case: a wooden *trapeza* with feet in the form of a griffon's head, and a little round co-vered basket finely woven of vegetable fibre, perhaps made to contain small objects of worth. On the left of the *fauces* are the stove, the latrine and the stairs leading to the upper floor. On the south side: an elegant *cubiculum*, with three skylights in the ceiling (two are recomposed) (PL. XXIV, *fig. 44*). At the end of the *atrium* lies the *triclinium*, with a few traces of the one–time luxurious decoration with black panels above a red dado. A glass case contains a number of strigils, a statuette of one of the Lares and a cup full of pine–seeds.

CASA DEL SACELLO IN LEGNO (*Insula V, n. 31*). – This house with a long, narrow ground–plan and of humble aspect still preserves the original distribution of rooms and traces of the more ancient decoration of a small house of the Republican era at Herculaneum (another example is the " Casa dell'erma in bronzo ,, , (*insula III, n. 16*). Besides several pavements in *opus signinum* with a geometrical design, there are some remains of the original noble decoration in the I style (imitation of marble revetments) on the architrave of the *tablinum*, on the internal wall of the *atrium* and elsewhere.

Above the *tablinum* there are the truncated shafts of the columns of an upper gallery like that in the stately " Casa Sanni-tica ,, of this same *insula* (*n. 1*). Behind the *tablinum*, there is on one side a drawing–room (*oecus*), with remains on the upper part of the wall of good decoration in the I style and in the III style on the lower part, whilst on the other side there is a simple store–room, where there were found many terra-cotta dolium–covers. In a *cubiculum* on the upper floor was found a great quantity of *tabulae ceratae*, some of them in a casket (*capsa*), others heaped together under the bed; unfortun-ately, their condition is such that it is extremely difficult, if not impossible, to read and interpret them.

In a room to the right of the *fauces* (in the form of an alcove, with a vaulted ceiling, and a grated window) was brought to light one of the most singular objects of ancient furniture, a *sacellum* in wood, that was at the same time cupboard and domestic *lararium*. The little, shrine, in the form of a small temple *in antis*, with the two Corinthian columns finely carved and fluted and its double doors opened, reveals to our gaze the statuettes of divinities within and in the lower section there still lie several objects of adornment, etc., belonging to the woman who must once have taken pleasure in its presence in her bedroom (PL. XXIII, *fig. 42*).

CASA CON GIARDINO (*Insula V, n. 33*). – It is a humble habitation with shop attached giving upon the street (*n. 32*). Long, narrow *fauces* with a small internal vestibule separate sufficiently the various rooms opening down one side only. These are mostly unadorned or bear traces of poor decoration with simple linear motifs. At the end there is a *cubiculum* with the remains of better wall–painting. On the left, on the corner formed by the *decumanus* and the *cardo*, where we should have expected to find a shop or some other locality of a commercial nature, there is a *hortus* which must have belonged originally to the more distinguished habitations beyond the walls, to the west (" Casa del gran portale „ and the Samnite house).

Turning the front of the insula on the decumanus inferior, we may visit the:

CASA DEL GRAN PORTALE (*Insula V, n. 8*). – The house is so–named from the beautiful portal with brick half–columns (originally stuccoed and painted red) surmounted by Corinthian capitals adorned with winged Victories, with an architrave decorated with guttae and mutules in terracotta; a portal that seems already to prelude, in the materials adopted and in the form, the later portarls of Roman houses at Ostia (PL. XXIII, *fig. 41*). Embedded in the walls of the *fauces* as constructional material there are tufa columns perhaps belonging to the ancient, destroyed peristyle of the adjoining " Casa sannitica „. The interior, though small and far from the traditional forms of the Pompeian house, indicates a certain financial ease.

The various rooms look out upon a covered vestibule, some of the full heigt, others with a low ceiling to allow for the upper storey; a small open courtyard, not in the centre but to the side of the entrance, on a higher level than the rooms, fulfils the double function of an *atrium*: to light and air the house and collect the rainwater from the roof into a cistern. The most important room in the house — *triclinium* and reception room — opens very near to the entrance. It has a fine painting of a Dionysian subject on the end wall; close by, there is an elegant little exedra with a frieze with curtains, Cupids and birds in flowering gardens. At the end of the vestibule is a well-decorated wall with slender architecture on a black ground and a little picture in the centre of birds pecking at butterflies and cherries. There is a very elegant room, overlooking the small courtyard, perhaps for the siesta with a good picture in marble *opus sectile* in the pavement and a pleasant motif of falling curtains in the wall decoration. The service quarters (larder, kitchen, latrine) are rationally disposed behind the reception rooms of the ground floor, where there is also to be found the staircase leading to the few rooms on the upper floor.

The *shop* (*n. 9*) beside the house but unconnected with it was probably let by the owner of the house, not managed personally by him.

In front of the " Casa del Gran Portale ,, , opens a series of shops belonging to the insula IV (*see p.* 56).

INSULAE ORIENTALES I ET II

The whole of the eastern quarter of the city lying between the extreme southern limit towards the shore and the cross-roads of the major *decumanus* may be divided into two great blocks of buildings, separated by a side street which does not corrispond with the arteries of the other quarters. The block on the south side still has the distinguished and luxurious character which we have observed in all the habitations along the sea-front, but the large block lying immediately to the north without the interruption of any street presents us with a physiognomy entirely new in the town architecture of Pompeii and Herculaneum. There is here a type of building that is highly developed both vertically and horizontally and divided into one or more apartments on each floor, such as we know so far only from the larger urban centres with a greater industrial and commercial development, like Ostia, Pozzuoli and Rome (PL. XXXIV, *fig. 61*).

The excavations on this side have been pushed as far as possible towards the entrance avenue and must later be continued still further on this front in order to reach the extreme limits of the oriental quarter of the city and the zone of the real suburban villas and the necropolis.

The road (*V cardo*), wider in the upper stretch (from the side street to the major *decumanus*), is paved with slabs of white, grey and veinned limestone right down to the last houses towards the shore; near to these it passes underneath the high brow of the residential quarters by means of an archway and descends rapidly down to the suburban quarter and to the sea (PL. XXXIX, *fig. 70*).

INSULA ORIENTALIS II

Although this *insula* is still in course of excavation, the part so far brought to light along the whole east front on the *V cardo* is sufficient to permit a summary outline of its general character: it is profoundly different not only from the other buildings of Herculaneum but from the types and forms of private edifices during the I century of the Empire, so copiously illustrated at Pompeii.

In place of the large distinguished dwellings or the small artisans' houses, which all have more or less in common with the traditional *domus*, we have here between the side street to the south and the major *decumanus* a grandiose building with a frontage of more than 80 metres, which, because of the uniform construction in the large, irregular *opus reticulatum* of the post–Augustan period, reinforced by jambs with alternate layers of brick and tufa, forms a homogeneous body of edificies of a single period, organically conceived. The widening and relaying of the road to be observed along this strech supports the idea that here we have the beginning of a real new quarter of the city and of a profound and radical transformation of town architecture, such as appears in full course of development during the II and III centuries of the Empire, especially at Ostia. Thus Herculaneum, even more than Pompeii, presents itselfs to us at the head of the revolutionary movement in the field of town architecture during the I century of the Empire, because of the more direct and immediate influence which the two great neighbouring centres of *Neapolis* and *Puteoli* must have exercised over it.

The two fronts of the *insula* present us with edifices of a different nature, built for different ends. On the *V cardo* front (towards the city) there is a series of houses of a more commercial character: shops and high blocks of flats with various entrances and entrance–stairs, all without any resemblance to the traditional house. On the east front of the *insula* facing the suburbs and the country there is (on a higher level) a series of magnificent vaulted rooms with apses and (on a lower level) a long porticoed *ambulacrum* opening upon a vast garden more than 80 metres long. The portico, the garden and the large rooms surrounding them are reached by two grandiose vestibules, each with a prostyle porch like that of a temple *in antis*, one of which lies upon the lesser *decumanus* and the other upon the major *decumanus*. The vastness of the peristyle and garden and the unusual grandeur of the entrances indicate the public character of the buildings and the area surrounded by a portico. The progress in the work of excavations have shown that this building was a public *Palaestra* or a *gymnasium*, the presence of which is testified by the remembrance of the *ludi gymnici*, in the honorary inscription on the marble base dedicated to Marcus Nonius Balbus (see p. 66) and strength ened by the existence, in Pompeii, of the wide *Palaestra* of imperial epoch, brought to light by the excavations of these last years.

The portico is reached across the magnificent entrance hall which, in the guise of a *propylon* or of a temple cella, faces with its two columns the eastern end of the lesser *decumanus* (*n. 4*). This edifice, traversed in various directions by the galleries of the underground excavations and summarily described by La Vega, was erroneously indicated as a " Temple of the *Mater Deum* ,, because of an inscription found in the neighbourhood which records the restoration of that temple by Vespasian (*C. I. L.*, X, 1406). The new excavations have shown that it is not a sacred edifice but the splendid entrance or *fauces* of a public area of the city. The entrance, composed of a *prothyron* with columns like the pronaos of a temple, and the vestibule (whose proportions are those of a great *tablinum*) had a black tessellated pavement with portions in marble *opus sectile*, whire walls with architectural decoration and a white vault, but the numerous perforations of the subterranean galleries caused the collapse of part of the walls and vaults, and the remains of their unusual decoration are arranged around the walls (PL. XXXV, *fig. 63*).

The parts of the peristyle and the garden now excavated are the ambulacrum and colonnade of the east wing: some of the tufa and brick Corinthian columns still lie thrown to the ground under the mud flow.

A great apsed room opens upon the middle of the portico wing and behind it, on a higher level, there are other large vaulted rooms still contaning part of their beautiful wall decoration with architectural motifs on a black ground.

The northern part of the zone is formed on the lower part by a windowed gallery (inside a long vaulted room) and above by a balcony, from which people watched the gymnastic exercises of the Herculaneum youths. The centre of the open area was crossed by a wide basin, its depth sufficient to be used as swimming–pool.

On a pilaster in the centre of the basin there has recently been replaced a large bronze fountain which was discovered during recent excavations: it consists of a tree trunk around which are entwined the large coils of a dragon–serpent: water spouted into the basin from the serpent's five heads.

Let us visit, now, in the lane flanking the Palaestra on the South, the

PISTRINUM (Bakery with oven and mills). – It is the first plant of the kind to be found in the area of the city so far disinterred and it must have been installed on the corner of the eastern *insula* (where several rooms belonging to a preceding house of a better class were coverted to this use) during the last years of the city's life (PL. XXXVI, *figg. 64–5*).

Immediately inside, there is the oven, with collapsed vault but with the iron door still closed, and near it there is a leaden tank in which to damp the straw broom used to clean the oven after baking. In the corner there are a large terracotta dolium and a basin made from part of a mill. In the tiny courtyard there are two mills of the usual type (*meta* and *catillus*); these were turned by asses, as is plainy demonstrated by the remains of bones found on the ground around by the bevelled angle of the pilaster (cut away to allow for the circulating of the animal) and by the presence of the stable (*stabulum*) for the shelter of beasts of burden. In the wall of the stable there are the deep sockets for the manger. On the other side of the court two small doors lead to two latrines separated by a partition. This baker of Herculaneum must indeed have prospered, if it were possible for him to unite to his *pistrinum* the distinguished vaulted rooms with fine tessellated pavements and the remains of good decoration which lie on a slightly higher level. In one of these rooms there is an elegant wooden table with the feet carved in the form of a griffon's head, once in an upper room.

But other interesting shops belong to the Insula orientalis II:

N. 1. – A large corner *shop*, with a backshop and the stone flag upon which rested the wooden staircase leading to the upper floor (*n. 5*).

N. 2. – Long *fauces* leading to the living quarters of the owner of the *pistrinum* in the south side street.

N. 3. – *Shop* arranged in the narrow interstice between two walls.

To the left of the great vestibule (*n. 4*), along the east pavement as far as the major *decumanus*, there is a whole series of large shop entrances and private doorways with stairs leading to upper storeys (not yet completely excavated).

N. 5. – *Workshop* (perhaps a dye–works) with a furnace made by removing the bottom from a *dolium* and cementing the latter to a stove. To the rear there is a backshop: above, a mezzanine and an upper floor.

N. 6. – *Shop* with a selling counter and the remains of decoration with a yellow ground. In the backshop there are amphorae both upright and upside down, inserted within one another.

N. 7. – Doorway and staircase leading to the upper floors of a large building divided into flats, a real main entrance to the modern type of house such as is to be found at Ostia.

N. 8. – Mill with bakery with four rooms, of which two opening on the street, in the shop two mills, in the back–shop 25 bronze baking–pans of every size. (In the glass–case standing against the wall is exhibited the seal of *Sex[ti] Patulci Felicis*, who probably was the proprietor of the bakery).

In dark sooty premises in the interior are to be found the perfectly preserved oven and the place for preparing pastry, both of them with the sign of the phallic emblem to ward off the evil spirits who were a threat to good baking.

N. 9. – *Shop* with a stove and a sink on one side and a *lararium* painting on the wall: *Hercules* pouring a libation between *Dionysos* and *Mercurius*.

N. 10. – *Shop* without a counter, probably belonging to an artisan. In the closed room a little loom, and a small bench near to it; upon the bed elegantly veneered with the motive of meanders, the skeleton of a youth; standing against the wall a marble table with the objects found in the excavation of the rooms of the ground and upper floor. As many gems were found in the back rooms, it has been supposed that this workshop belonged to a *gemmarius*.

N. 11. – Dye house with furnace: in the back room a *trápeza*.

N. 12. – Entrance hall connecting the shops *n. 11* and *13*.

N. 13. – *Shop* with xounter (cereals and vegetables; corn and beans); in the glass–case some silver rings and a seal with the name *A(uli) Fuferi*.

N. 14–16. – *Workshops* of artisans; in *n. 16* is preserved one of the wooden folds of the back room.

N. 17. – Entrance and staircase leading to the dwellings of the upper floor.

N. 18. – *Workshop* (perhaps a dye–works), with a furnace placed between two big counters.

N. 19. – Imposing hall with two columns on the front. The pavement was of black *tesserae* and marble; at present traces only remain of the sparkling wall decoration in IV style, and of the marble socle. Almost in the centre, the hall is divided into two parts by slender columns and pillars. The *fauce* opening on the southern part leads to the gallery placed upon the wide *Palaestra* (see p. 53); along the gallery open two vaulted rooms elegantly decorated and others rustic.

Let us, now, return, to the insula IV, to complete the visit of the shops on the decumanus inferior:

Shop *n. 10*, House, *n. 11.* – The selling–counter is not placed before the opening, as is usual at Pompeii, but in the inner corner. The large quantity of carbonized or rather mineralized grain found in a *dolium* suggests that the chief stock of this shop were cereals. The adjoining room to the east must have served as a backshop and living room. The mean dwelling with its entrance at *n. 11* was connected with this shop: on the left, there is a corridor with a latrine at the end, and a large room with two windows and tye remains of elegant decoration on the upper part of the wall; on the right, with a very low doorway, there is a *cubiculum* with a few traces of white stucco decoration.

House *n. 12–13.* – This is the entrance to the home of the owner of the great shop at the crossing of the *decumanus* with the *cardo* (*n. 15–16*, see below): the habitation embraces all ehe rooms between the private entrance *n. 12* and the shop tntrance at *n. 15*, with the exception of the shop *n. 14* which is wedged with its two floors into the larger edifice and seems rather to have belonged to a wine merchant than to have been the *caupona* of a small retailer, to judge by the large number of amphorae found there (Pl. XXIX, *fig. 52*).

The entrance at *n. 13* (also fianked by a small shop or office for the settlement of business negotiations) opens into a vestibule with two low well–heads on a level with the pavement; above one of these was recovered a wooden windlass for drawing water. Nearby, there are two cubicles for the door–keeper.

The small rectangular *atrium* (with the marble—edged *impluvium* tank and the *opus signinum* pavement adorned with *tesserae* and segments of marble), together with the two well—decorated rooms facing one another, form the real family quarters of the rich merchant. The *sectile* square wihch decorates the pavement of the small *triclinium* to the south of *atrium* is noteworthy for the delicate, precious detail. The corridor at the end of the *atrium* connected the house with the shop.

SHOP *n. 15–16.* – It is the largest and richest shop so far discovered at Herculaneum, with two wide entrances, the larger one on the *decumanus*, the smaller on the *cardo*. The selling—counter, with a double podium faced with polychrome marble fragments, is well inside the shop, so as to offer shelter and rest to customers instead of compelling them to remain on the pavement outside. There are eight *dolia* fixed into the base of the counter, containing cereals and vegetables; another larger *dolium* is half—buried in a pilaster. There is a cooking stove in the south—east corner (PL. XXIX, *fig. 53*). Behind the shop, there are two backshops separated by a sliggh partition in *opus craticium;* to the side are store rooms and offices formed by the merchant out of the finely decorated rooms of the original habitation. The position of the shop at an important cross—roads, near to a public fountain, must have made the fortune of the proprietor and it explains the excellent furnishing of the shop itself, and the spaciousness of the living quarters attah ched to it.

At the corner of the lesser decumanus *and the* cardo, *leaning against the pavement and partly embedded in it, there is a*

PUBLIC FOUNTAIN, called the fountain of *Neptune* from the rough mask adorning the water—spout. Like the many fountains of Pompeii, it is composed of a simple rectangular basin with a head in which is fixed the conducting *fistula*, the mouth being ornamented by an emblematic mask. The basin is formed of large limestone slabs held together by leaden cramps. The sculpture, though rude, is full of the sound, simple vigour of popular art and there is a certain deliberate facetiousness in the expression of the deity from between whose lips issues the water—jet (PL. III, *fig. 6*).

Continuing along the front the same insula:

HABITATION AND SHOP *n. 17–18.* – This house, like the the preceding ones, is quite spacious but simple, almost rustic, in character. At one side there is a hop (*n. 17*), with a communicating door between it and the actual dwelling; it is a habitation of people of the commercial classes but their business was less prosperous than that of the great corner shop and there sfore it has a more modest air.

The rather small shop has a counter just inside the threshold, upon which are exposed nuts (recovered from the great *dolium* half-buried in the ground), some bronze utensilis and two lamps; near to the entrance there are the remains of a fireplace. On the wall behind the counter there is painted a Priapic figure, a large round-bellied *dolium* and a female figure with a *tintinnabulum* and a purse in her hands, all emblems against the evil eye. The little room behind served as a backshop and store room; it has a low *podium* all round and there are the holes made for the wooden shelf-supports; higher up there is to be seen the painted dado of a room on the upper floor, with green bushes on a white ground. A leaden water tank was found in this room.

The house (*n. 18*) has long *fauces* divided by a slight partition wall (perhaps for the construction of the staircase leading to the upper floor); then it unfolds itself normally around a little tetrastyle *atrium* closed by a *pluteus*, or parapet, with a windowed gallery above, upon which opened almost all the rooms on the first floor, so that the *atrium* fulfills the function of a light-well, like that in the " Casa a graticcio „. The rooms, ruined by the underground galleries, retain but little of the original decoration. The *triclinium* which opens upon the east side of the *atrium* with little paintings of fish and marine animals on the walls is worthy of notice; it is preceded by a small anteroom. A little opening, like a spy-hole, in the wall towards the shop bears witness to the wary surveillance of the owner of the house over the person who managed the shop for him.

CASA DELLA STOFFA *n. 19-20*. – The dwelling and workshop of artisans, possibly either cloth-makers or cloth-merchants. In the simple room at the entrance, used as a shop, there are a stove, a dozen amphorae and a large mortar. Adjoining this, there is a large room with the remains of painting in the IV style. To the rear lies a small room where there are shown pieces of material, their design still recognizable. Finally, a short corrior leads to several rooms and a latrine illuminated by a light-well. The arrangement of the stairs is unusual in this house: there is a large staircase with a street entrance that leads to the upper floor and beneath it a smaller one leads up from the shop to a mezzanine room.

CASA DEI CERVI (*Insula IV, n. 21*). – After the series of humble abodes and shops of merchants and artisans along the *decumanus* and the *V cardo*, the *insula* terminates on the south (as on the opposite side of the *IV cardo*) with a large distinguished dwelling, the richest, most luxurious an most rationally constructed of all the rich and beautiful houses along the south front. The edifice occupies a vast rectangular area 43 metres long and may be divided into two principal parts: the northern entrance quarter and the southern quarter of the terraces, connected with one another by means of a *quadriporticus* with windows. The structure and the decoration are of the period of Claudius and Nero (*fig. 5*).

The entrance, ennobled only by the stretch of marble pavement, leads to the small covered (testudinate) *atrium*, here serving as a vestibule upon which open the other rooms, like the anteroom of a modern house. From one side is reached the great *triclinium* and the *quadriporticus*, and on the other a corridor behind the *triclinium* leads to the internal part of the house, the kitchen and the larder. Above, there are the simple servant's quarters, reached by a small staircase and a wooden gallery.

The spacious *triclinium* and drawing–room, with its walls austerely painted from dado to cornice with sober architectural and ornamental motifs on a black ground broken by wide red bands, has on the other hand a dazzling pavement of marble intarsia work, without any real geometrical design, being composed of so many separate tiles of varying shapes in different marbles. Originally, from the great open portal of the portico the view streched out across the garden and the *pergula* on the terrace to the sea (PL. XXX, *figs. 54–55*).

The two groups of deer attacked by hounds to be seen in this room were found together with the other sculptures now in other parts of the house, in a part of the garden not traversed by underground galleries. The exquisite, nervous sensibility of the modelling places them amongst the most beautiful animal groups we possess of Pompeian and Herculanean sculpture (PL. XXXII, *fig. 58*).

On the same side there are: a small room leading to the kitchen, the *apotheca* and the latrine, and a beautiful internal *cubiculum* with red walls an a pavement in marble *sectile*; in the rear there is an elegant reception room (*oecus*) with the walls and the vault finely painted with, a red ground and a polychrome marble floor. In the centre, there is a charming statuette of the *Satyr with a wineskin*, a variant of the other famous bronze statuette found at Pompeii (PL. XXI, *fig. 56*; XXII, *fig. 57*).

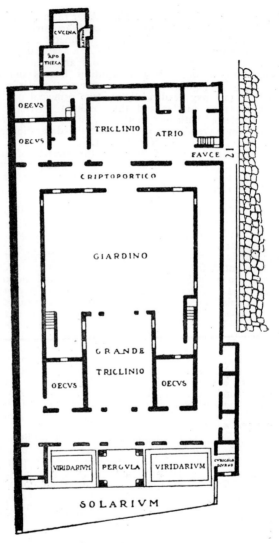

FIG. 5 — CASA DEI CERVI

The ample *quadriporticus*, having lost the architectonic element of the columns which still survives in the adjoining " Casa dell'atrio a mosaico ,, (see p. 27), assumes the more rational and convenient form of a corridor with windows, just as is found in a present–day house, whilst it preserves the dignified wall decoration and that of the pavement, whose divisions corrispond to the openings in the walls, the windows. The charming little pictures that still survive inserted in the panels on the walls, with scenes of *Cupids playing*, belong to a longer series of picture detached during the preceding excavations and is now preserved in the Naples Museum (PL. XXXIII, *figs 59–60*). The garden, closed between the walls of the *quadriporticus* and adorned with marble tables and sculptures, is still adorned at the *triclinium* end by a great portal with a pediment once entirely reveted with glass–paste mosaic, with a head of *Oceanus* in the centre of a frieze of *Cupids on hippocampi*. The capital with a baroque flavour, with marble intarsia on ardesian stone, either belonged to a shrine now destroyed or else it was carried here from some other edifice by the violent rush of water.

The south quarters, between the garden and the terraces opening upon the view of the shore and the gulf, are still more sumptuous, though less well preserved. In the centre there is a room which served as a summer *triclinium* and *oecus*; unfortunately only a small part of the pavement in *opus sectile* escaped the saking of the " cunicoli ,, , and little remains of the decoration (a still–life and a mythological or tragic painting on the corner pilaster). This room is flanked by two beautiful smaller ones, with windows looking into the garden and marble pavements. In the middle of the loggia there is a *pergula* with four pilasters (the terracotta vases beside the latter are original) and on either side there is a room for repose and for the siesta (*diaetae*); one of these has superb remains of an *opus sectile* pavement. Beyond, there was an uncovered terrace (*solarium*).

In the room on the east side there is a statuette, powerfully and vigorously modelled, of the *drunken Hercules*. Roman art has jokingly represented the god who founded the city not in one of his heroic undertakings but as the victim of his exorbitant indulgence in wine: with his paunch dilaed like a wineskin, a stupified expression on his face, unsteady legs and his club slung carelessly across his shoulder, the hero accomplishes the least heroic act of his life: that of passing water.

It is formed by two houses only, *n. 1-2*, the " Casa della Gemma ,, and the " Casa del rilievo di Telefo ,, , which although they open with their *atria* upon the *V cardo*, are planned with their longest axis from north to south (like the " Casa dell'Albergo ,, , the " Casa dell'atrio a mosaico ,, and the " Casa dei Cervi ,,) in order to overlook thea sea with their terraces. The larger and more sumptuous of the two houses, the " Casa del rilievo di Telefo ,, (*n. 2*) is particularly instructive: it almost surrounds the above–lying " Casa della Gemma ,, and then spreads out with its luxurious apartments towards the view of the sea. Both houses, constructed as they are on the extreme edge of the hill, have utilized the fall in the ground for the creation of loggias, store rooms and other localities below the street–level of the city: the disinterment of these rooms, still incomplete, may perhaps offer us precious elements for the study of these two beautiful habitations (PL. XXXV, *fig. 63*).

We cross the road from the " Casa dei Cervi ,, and enter the:

CASA DELLA GEMMA (*Insula orientalis I, n. 1*), so–called from a gem engraved with a female head of the Claudian period discovered in it. In the Tuscan *atrium*, with magnificent decoration in red and black, finely executed and forming a harmonious whole, there is the unusual arrangement of walls reinforced by pilasters for the support of the roof and of a *prostylon* near the *tablinum*, which here opens upon a *cubiculum* at the rear and upon a terrace originally closed by pilasters and windows (PL. XXXVII, *fig. 66*). On the right of the *atrium* a curved passage leads to the kitchen and the latrine. The light and airy, well–preserved kitchen (on the fireplace there is a kettle and another cylindrical vessel for boiling water, which must have been inserted into the stove found on the same spot) opens upon a small terrace. On the wall of the latrine an irreverent servant recorded the visit made there by a famous physycian: *Apollinaris medicus Titi imperatoris*.

At the end of the *atrium* are a vestibule and a corridor (a black mosaic with white bands) which lead to a large apartment and other airy, luminous rooms of the terrace quarters. The great mosaic square with a fine geometrical design imitating the textile art of carpet–making that decorates the pavement of the noble and airy apartment used as a *triclinium* and drawing-room is worthy of examination. The two rooms (*alcova* and anteroom) to the left of the corridor were also finely decorated.

There are to be glimpsed the rooms of the cellar–floor of the house. The great external uncovered loggia has here also two rooms for repose from which to delight in the view, despoiled of their decoration.

CASA DEL RILIEVO DI TELEFO (*Insula orientalis I, n. 2–3*). – Taken as a whole, including the area occupied by the servants' quarters and the garden which reaches to the side street on the east (entrance at *n. 3*), this habitation forms one of the richest and most extensive abodes of the southern quarter of the city, notwithstanding the fact that the desire to look out together with the other lordly dwellings over the panorama of the gulf, the sudden steep slope of the ground and the respect for the adjoining " Casa della Gemma ,, all combined to compel the owner to create an abnormal ground–plan, with a strong oblique divergence in relation to the main axis of the *insula*.

Thus, the *atrium* quarter is on the same level as the street, whilst the peristyle quarter is on a lower level the two parts being connected with each other by means of a ramp. The good preservation of the pavement and the scanty preservation of the walls and their decoration show that more damage was caused by the violent impetus of the muddly alluvion, which overthrew and dragged after it in its ruinous path all that stood in the way of its flow towards the sea, than by the tunnelling.

On either side of the entrance there is a beautiful *relief with a quadriga in motion;* these have been recomposed from fragments found partly in this house and partly in other houses along the *V cardo*, a sign that they belonged, together with other reliefs recovered during the old excavations of the Bourbon period and now in foreign museums, to a possibly public edifice in the central quarter of the city from which they were detached and deposited here and there by the muddy lava current.

The *atrium*, without fauces and with colonnades at the sides in two minor aisles, calls to mind by its graceful architectonic composition the forms of the so–called *oeci corinthii*, that is, noble porticoed rooms. The roof (of the Tuscan type) was on a level with the upper floor. The marble *oscilla* with satyric figures and theatrical masks, suspended between the columns as in the " Casa degli Amorini ,, at Pompeii, stand out admirably from the glossy red background of the walls and columns (PL. XXXVIII, *fig. 68*). Other minor marble panels and *oscilla*, some of them bearing vigorously carved Satyrs and Sileni (PL. XXXVII, *fig. 67*), are to be seen in a glass case in the left wing near to the *podium* of a shrine (they were found in the rooms above the *atrium*), together with various household objects, including a precious necklace of amulets, several lamps and various remains of comestibles, such as bread, small cakes and eggs.

On the north side of the *atrium* two small doors lead from the living quarters to the *stabulum*, which had its own independent street entrance (*n. 3*) with the usual ramp for the passage of small carts and beasts of burden. The *stabulum* or *equile* (stable) is easily recognizable in the rectangular room with a low ceiling that backs upon the *atrium* wall.

A steeply sloping corridor leads to the part of the house buit upon a lower level: the great, luxurious quarter of the peristyle and the terraces, together with a few other localities. The peristyle with brick columns encloses a garden surrounded by the low walls of a *pluteus*, with a rectangular tank faced with blue plaster in the middle. Part of the garden area which lies above the still-interred subterranean rooms is paved by a stratum of *bipedales*, in order better to protect the underlying cellars from the infiltration of rain and soil. To the south of the peristyle there are three more or less richly decorated rooms with the remains of paintings, of marble dados and pavements in *opus sectile* and mosaic: behind them, at the end of the corridor which continues the ambulacrum of the peristyle, there is an open terrace with several rooms opening upon it. The largest and most splendid of these rooms on the extreme southern limits of the house is that which has restored to us the most magnificent marble decoration ever found in a private house of antiquity and worthy of an imperial palace. The room (9.20 m. by 6.60 m.) has its chief entrance on the side of the loggia and, besides the rich polychrome marble pavement, it has a sumptuous dado faced with great horizontal and vertical panels of " cipollino ,, , " pavonazzetto ,, and " africano ,, marble, framed by bands and interrupted by spiral-fluted half-columns with Corinthian capitals. Of the precious whole, it has been possible to reconstruct the dado of one of the walls; the rest was carried away by the fury of the alluvion. All the decoration may be said to be of the Flavian period (PL. XXXVIII, *fig. 69*).

In one of the smaller rooms that precede the rich drawing room there was found a charming neo-Attic relief representing the myth of *Telephus*, which, because of the somewhat cold and academic accuracy of the composition, forms one of the most representative productions in the eclectic classicized manner of the late Hellenistic schools. The garden to the north of this habitation, which must have been a late addition, hides here and there in the subsoil the remains of preceding constructions. Here, roughly attached to the boundary wall, there is the rustic shrine dear to the servant who had charge of this humble part of dwelling.

This house, taking vantage of the low level of the ground, displayed its rooms on the lower floor like the ' House of the Albergo '. These rooms, as those of the upper floor, preserve a rich decoration: under the sumptuous hall with marble pavement and walls, another one was built, with finer marble pavement and the walls decorated with one of the most elaborate ornamental composition known in the Herculanean paintings. The gallery on the eastern side of this hall, with half–columns and windows, leading to the other rooms of the house (not yet excavated), is to be noted.

SUBURBAN QUARTER

The high wall with bastions of the patrician dwellings of the southern front (Houses of Argo, Albergo, Atrio a mosaico, the Cervi, Gemma, Rilievo di Telefo) marks the edge of the promontory on which the city has been built, and the line of the ancient city walls towards the sea. The city walls are partly to be recognized from the structures uncovered after the fall of the rough–cast. The excavations of these last years along the whole front of this wall, not only have marked the line of the city between the two gates opening at the end of the cardines IV and V, but has also brought to light the first suburban quarters of the city, which, outside of the walls, had to develope more or less without interruption as far as the harbour, and to form here the maritime suburban quarter of Herculaneum. Unfortunately two facts make the excavations here more difficult and slower than elsewhere: the extreme hardness of the solidified mud, which in this part of the city assumes the aspect of a stone bank, harder than the usual volcanic tufa; secondly the phenomenon of the bradisysmus, i. e. of the slow falling of the coast–line: for this phenomenon the pavements of the buildings which, before 79 A. D. doubtelessly were on a dry ground, at present are under the level of the ground waters, for a depth approssimatively of 1.50 metres. These circumstances will oblige the excavators to limit the development of their work till adequate installment for the isolation and drying up of the waters, will be arranged. Notwithstanding these difficulties, in past times many attempts have been made to fix by means of sondation wells the form of the ancient shore and its distance from the city. At present, this distance is about 300 mt., but in ancient times it was less.

Bearing in mind the present configuration of the land and the line of the sounding wells it may be gathered that along the axis of greatest depth it did not exceed 400 metres, cuving and approaching the inhabited quarters by 150 to 200 metres and forming the two inlets respectively to the East and to the West which have today disappeared under the enormous alluvional mass of eruptive material.

Going out through the Gate of the *cardo V*, which we may call Porta Marina, as in ancient times the harbour and the Marine were reached through it, and following the steep narrow slope just at the city walls, we reach the suburban zone of the ancient city built on a marshy ground, on account of the infiltration of the waters. From this point started the road leading to the harbour and to the shore. And, as at Pompeii, also here we find the first tombs, reserved to the most notorious citizens in the public area.

BASES DEDICATED TO M. NONIUS BALBUS. – Two marble bases stand on the square; one of them, the smaller, had to support a statue dedicated to the proconsul *M. Nonius Balbus;* but till now only the head of this statue has been recovered (traces of the feet are to be seen on the plan of the base. (The other base, the bigger one, having the form of a funeral altar, preserves an inscription telling us of the honours to be attributed to the same M. Nonius Balbus, one of the most famous citizens of Herculaneum. Among the honours, is mentioned the erection of an equestrian statue (this statue was found in the Basilica and is now exhibited in the National Museum of Naples).

SUBURBAN BATHS. – Built against the edifices of the " Casa della Gemma ,, e " del rilievo di Telefo ,, there is a big square building, with a beautiful stuccoed and painted portal. Owing to the characteristic shape of the rooms, to the illumination from above by sky–lights, to the presence of double walls for the conveyance of hot air, it is easy to realise that this was a public Therma. Surely these public Baths were built after those placed near the Forum. The excavations, still in course, present great difficulties on account of the nature of the earth and above all of the presence of the water. Very interesting, from an architectural point of view, is the entrance hall, lighted up by a shaft supported by four pillars with little contrasting arches.

In the long building extending towards the west beneath the " Casa dell'Atrio a mosaico ,, and the " Casa dell'Albergo ,, the wing of a courtyard may be discerned flanked by vaulted rooms and by two *Chapels* one of which appears to be covered by a sloping roof. These were probably the premises of some religeous corporation in the immediate outskirts of the city.

THE THEATRE

This is the only edifice still visible belonging to the first period of excavation. Those who desire, after the sight of the disinterred quarters of the city, to have an unforgettable impression of the dramatic and sometimes heroic daring of the dark work carried out by means of wells and galleries, must visit the ancient theatre of the city. In the last few years this has been rendered more conveniently accessible by the installation of an electric–light plant, although a more complete notion of the scheme of the edifice is to be gained from the study of the data and the repeated plans made of it than from the incomplete sight of the theatre itself (*fig. 6*; PL. XL, *fig. 71*).

personages (five of them were recovered and are now in the Naples Museum) and decorated architectonically by three niches flanked by bronze equestrian statues, of which unfortunately only fragments have been recovered. The façade of the *scaena* was rich in rare polychrome marbles before being vandalously sacked and despoiled by Prince d'Elboeuf. It seems that here all the art of the Herculanean marble workers, already admired in the pavements and walls of the town houses, must have gone to make of this stage–wall an admirable example of chromatic and decorative magnificence of the kind dear to the taste of Campanian craftsmen, with columns of " giallo antico ,, , " cipollino ,, and " africano ,, and revetment slabs of " rosso porfifico ,, , alabaster and " pavonazzetto ,,: a taste that will survive and reappear triumphantly in the polychrome decoration of the churches and chapels of the most beautiful Neapolitan baroque period. Together with the marble revetments were dispersed the sculptures from the stage–wall, amongst which were the " Grande ,, and the " Piccola Ercolanese ,, , now exiled in the Dresden Museum.

The edifice, as is to be seen from its structure, is all of the Roman era, of the Augustan and post–Augustan periods, whilst the decoration is of the time of Claudius and Nero. An inscription, at one time repeated above the varius entrances to the theatre, attributes the construction to the private generosity of *Lucius Annius Mammianus Rufus, duumvir,* and the architect *Numisius.*

After the ill-fated plundering of d'Elboeuf, unhappily of long duration (from 1709 to 1738), the first person to recognize the nature of the edifice and to prevent its further il-treatment was De Venuti (1738), who pointed out his discovery to the Bourbon king, Charles III. The excavation by means of subterranean galleries was commenced in the same year, 1738, under the guidance first of all of Alcubierre, then of Weber until 1765 and, finally, of La Vega until 1777, with the praiseworthy intention to draw up plans and elevations and make an architectural study of the edifice and render it permanently accessible. The many elevations then made led to different architectural solutions regarding the more obscure parts of the monument, such as the *scaena* and the corona of the *cavea*, and to the construction of a not altogether trust-worthy plastic model under the guidance of Ruggiero, which has been brought up to date in the last few years and is now exhibited in the lower vestibule of the Theatre entrance.

But whilst wandering and turning about in the damp network of galleries which traverses the *cavea* and the orchestra without being able to see the building as a whole, it is impossible not to think, though admiring the patient, heroic work of engineers and workers, that it would have taken less time and perhaps less money to excavate and isolate the edifice from its bank of mud and restore the completest ancient theatre in Italy to the light of the sun.

Entrance: open during the same hours as the new excavations.

The entrance to the Theatre may be reached either by leaving the new excavations from the exit on *Corso Ercolano* and following the road in the direction of Naples or by walking up from te lower exit of the excavations by the populous and

The theatre of Herculaneum rose on the margin of the north-east residential quarters, near a temple and in the midst of an area that may have been connected with the Forum of the city. Thus the hemicycle of the *cavea*, instead of being cut into the hillside like the theatre of Pompeii, was a construction (like the ancient theatre of Naples and Roman theatres in general) supported upon a double order of arches and pilasters with 19 arches to each order. The arches, entablature and columns were all decorated with an elegant revetment of stucco and painting in the last Pompeian style. Two flights of stairs led from the two extremities of the lower portico to the corridor of the *media cavea* and other minor stairs led to the upper order. In the *cavea* there were the following divisions: the four wide tiers of the *ima cavea* for the seats

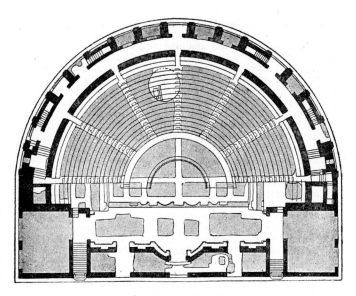

FIG. 6 – PLAN OF THE THEATRE

(*subsellia*) of the magistrates and other worthy citizens; sixteen tiers of seats which formed the *media cavea* divided into six sections (*cunei*) by seven flights of steps (*scalaria*) cut raywise into the thickness of the tiers; finally, separated by a parapet (*balteus*) about one metre high, there were the three tiers of *summa cavea*. Above the entrances to the orchestra there were the *tribunalia*, real separate boxes with independent entrances for the authorities and other personages. Since the radius of the hemicycle is shorter than that of the great theatre of Pompei (53 metres instead of 62) and the number of the seats in the *cavea* is also smaller, it may be calculated that the theatre held from 2500 to 3000 spectators at the most; a theatre in reasonable proportion to the number of inhabitants, which cannot have been more than about 4–5000.

The crest of the wall of the *summa cavea* was crowned by bronze statues, larger than life–size, of emperors and municipal popular *Vico a Mare* to the *Corso*. The upper entrance lies amidst the houses of modern Resína built over the *cavea;* an inscription of 1865 records the last improvements made upon it.

From the lower vestibule a flight of 72 steps cut into the tufa bank (which because of its solidity and the water which oozes from the walls has assumed almost the aspect of stone) leads down to the upper part of the theatre (*summa cavea*), recognizable from the double flights of steps that descend to the great circular ambulacrum between the *summa* and the *media cavea*; the latter is traversable from one extremity to the other, where there are the stairs leading down to the level of the orchestra. Seven *vomitoria* with arched doorways open towards the tiers of the *cavea*, which are formed by wide and comfortable steps in trachitic stone. Upon the semicircular wall surrounding the uppermost tier there are still to be seen traces of the rough—coating bed of the original marble facing. The descent is made by the central flight of steps lit by a great circular light well to the area of the orchestra, where there are interspersed great supporting pylons cut into the tufaceous mass of mud flow. The orchestra now lies 26.60 metres below the level of the modern *Corso Ercolano*. Before us is the front of the *proscaenium* of the usual type, with round and square niches deprived of their decoration and minor sculptures. At the two extremities of *proscaenium*, near the pilasters of the main entrances to the orchestra (*paradoi*), there remain the bases of two honorary statues (the statues either were never found or were removed during the first disordered plunderings of d'Elboeuf).

One base with the inscription:

M. NONIO M. F. BALBO

PR. PROCOS.

HERCVLANENSES

testifies the public gratitude of the city to that *Marcus Nonius Balbus*, proconsul of Crete and Cirenaica, who was amongst the most worthy citizens of Herculaneum and of whom we possess the equestrian statue found together with others of the same family in another public edifice, the so—called Basilica.

The other is dedicated:

AP. CLAVDIO C. F. PVLCHRO

COS. IMP.

HERCVLANENSES POST MORTEM

that is, to *Appius Claudius Pulcher*, who was consul in the year 38 B. C. (?) and must have acquired uncommon merit in the eyes of the citizens of Herculaneum in order to have been found worthy of the great honour of a commemorative statue on the front of the *proscaenium* of the theatre.

Upon ascending one of the little side—stairs which put the orchestra in communication with the *pulpitum,* there are still to be glimpsed the skeletal remains of the mural structure of whrat was once the magnificent architectonic façade of the *scaena.* There is a large doorway flanked by propylon in the central apsidal curve; on either hand is another doorway and signs of upper rectangular niches. There still remain several fine capitals, their *càlathos* carved with the leaves of water-plants, which must have surmounted the columns of precious polychrome marbles belonging to the upper order. Behind the *scaena,* where the edifice for the convenience of the public opened into a porticoed square (*porticus post scaenam*), as at Pompeii and elsewere, there are traces of the fine revetments of the pilasters and walls of the blind arches. (The imprint in the hardened mud indicated by the guides of the place as that of a mask was probably the impress made in the still—liquid mud by one of the statues of the *scaena* or of the portico). The external gallery to the right of the *scaena* is followed and the first archway leading to the orchestra is passed (here the beautiful painted and stuccoed decoration of the pilaster is almost intact), then through a second archway, one of the side staircases leading to the upper ambulacrum is ascended; thence, to the exit.

APPENDIX

THE VILLA SUBURBANA DEI PAPIRI. — Although since its definite abandonment in 1765, with the closing of the galleries and ventilation wells invaded by the insidious and deadly mephitic exhalations, the " Villa suburbana dei Papiri ,, has remained inaccessible and buried anew beneath its double stratum of mud—lava of 79 A. D. and fire—lava of 1631, nevertheless, its discovery and the consequent marvellous recuperation of works of art and papyri is so closely bound up with the history and destiny of Herculaneum that it will not be out of place to make a few remarks upon it, with the aid of the exact plan made of it by its meritorious excavator: Charles Weber (s. *fig.* 7).

The Villa lay with its front more than 250 metres long (the length of the city *decumanus*) parallel to the line of the coast, to the west of the city between the actual *Via Cécere*

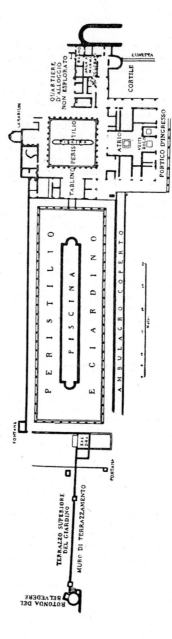

FIG. 7 – PLAN OF THE GREAT "VILLA SUBURBANA DEI PAPIRI,,

and the *Vico a Mare*, in the area of the gardens of the Augusti-
nian Fathers: an area invaded in 1631 by the lave which descended as far as the Granatello promontory. It must have
enjoyed the widest and freest possible view from its happy
position half—way up the slopes of this last flank of Vesuvius,
where no other constructions impeded the outlook and where
it lay beside its garden closed by a colonnade with vast vineyards,
vegetable gardens and a wood spread out before it down to the
tiny port necessary to its approach from the sea. The coast—
road which bounded it towards Vesuvius assured it of the most
direct and convenient means of communication with *Neapolis*
and the other cities, villages and villas on the gulf. Constructed on the hard bank of ancient, prehistoric lava, protected
from the icy north winds by the woody slopes of Vesuvius,
cooled by the west winds (which according to Strabo made
Herculaneum a most salubrious city), lying halfway between
sea and mount, withdrawn but not isolated, tranquil but not
cut off from the possibility of a rapid service of couriers and
news—bearers, with the double benefit of the climate of sea
and hill and, above all, the delight of one of the most grandiose
and harmonious panoramas for the satisfaction of the completely
Roman passion for views over sea and shore, this villa must
have been the ideal residence for the distinguished, cultured
patrician who loved to alternate the serene contemplation of the
beauty of nature with meditation and interior spiritual reflection.

There has been much discussion as to the proprietorship of
this Villa, without being able to leave the field of more or less
possible hypotheses. Certainly the singular circumstance of
the presence in the villa of many works of the Epicurean philosopher *Philodemus* renders extremely verisimilar the theory
of Comparetti, that is, that there should be some relation between the owner of the Villa and the author most represented
in the papyrus library. Since, according to an oration of Cicero, the friend and protector of the Epicurean *Philodemus*
was *L. Calpurnius Piso Cesoninus*, the father—in—law of Julius
Caesar and bitterest enemy of Cicero, it was reasonably de-
ducted that the suburban Villa of Herculaneum belonged
to *L. Calpurnius Piso* and to his direct descendents during
the Augustan and Imperial period, and that the library of a
prevailingly philosophical character were that chosen and
collected by his philosopher friend, *Philodemus* of Gadara. It
is to be excluded, however, that the owner is to be recognized,
as Comparetti sustained, in one of the most admirable bronze
portraits found in the Villa, in the so—called pseudo—Seneca,
though it seems rather to be the portrait of a Greek comic
poet, perhaps Philemon.

Although of such gigantic proportions in comparison with the other villas discovered so far in the Vesuvian region (the " Villa di Diomede ,, and the " Villa dei Misteri ,, , at Pompeii), the Villa remains faithful in its plan and the arrangement of the different parts to the fundamental architectural and constructional scheme of the suburban villa of the Pompeian and Stabian countryside. The atrium is reduced, that is, from being the vital centre of the Italic and Roman house, to the more modest function of a more or less rich entrance vestibule, separating the various quarters of the house. The real dwelling and reception quarters are distributed around the peristyle and terraces in order to enjoy more directly the light and heat of the sun and the view of fields and sea. Finally, a third essential element was the ample garden area, both covered and uncovered, for exercice in the shade or in the fortifying heat of the sun (*solarium*). These various elements are clearly to be gathered from Weber's plan, although the excavation of the east side was left unfinished and thus we cannot yet knkow the edifice as a whole. The incomplete exploration of the discovered area has revealed nothing to us of the agricultural and maritime side of the Villa's systematization. However, on the basis of the plan and the diary of the excavations and discoveries it is possible to offer a summary description of the interior (see *Plan, fig.* 7).

The entrance and atrium quarter. – The entrance faced the sea with a columned porch. Wide *fauces*, already of a vestibule nature, lead to the *atrium* (black and white mosaic pavement) with the *impluvium* tank surrounded by 11 fountain statues (*Sileni* pouring water from a wine–skin and *Cupids* pouring it from the mouth of a dolphin); other statues and busts in the niches in the *atrium* walls.

The first peristyle quarter. – A square peristyle with 10 columns to each side, and a long, narrow *impluvium* tank in the middle; in each corner a conch shell fountain and a bronze *herma* (amongst the hermae were those of the *Doryphorus* and the *Amazon*); at the end of the ambulatory there is a square room (an *oecus–triclinium ?*) and an apsed room (Lararium?).

The living quarter. – It lay to the east of the peristyle, exposed partly to the north and partly towards a sunny internal court. A bath was found here, rather small, as are all the villa baths of the close of the Republic and the beginning of the reign of Augustus. In an equally small room, there was discovered the precious library of carbonized papyrus rolls,

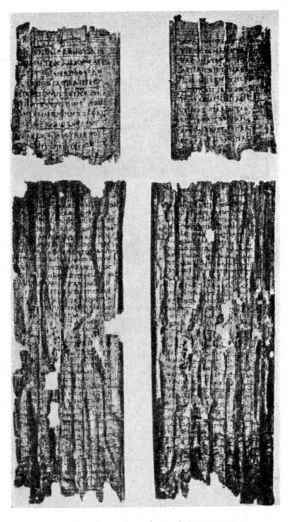

FIG. 8 - FRAGMENTS OF HERCULANEAN PAPYRI

some of them arranged upon shelves around the room and others upon the two sides of a central bookstand (*fig. 8*). Adjoining, there are stately reception rooms and studies with marble intarsia pavements.

The great peristyle quarter. – To the west of the first peristyle, across a spacious *tablinum* in which stood the archaistic statue of *Athena prómachos* beneath a *propylaeum*, there was the exit to the grandiose garden peristyle, as wide and airy as the *Forum* and the public *Palaestra* of a city (100 metres by 37 metres): the tank in the centre (66 metres by 7 metres) had the vast proportions of a *stagnum* or one of the great *natationes* of the imperial baths of the metropolis.

Along the *ambulacrum* of the peristyle, in the intercolumnar spaces and also in the open part of the garden and upon the borders of the great tank, there was found a real gallery of works of art: statues, busts, *hermae*, and small sculptures in marble and bronze, chosen with the eclectic taste of a connoisseur and lover of the arts. The works range from archaic art to the animal groups interspersed amongst the verdure of the avenues. They include the group of the so–called *Dancing Women*, the *Sleeping Faun*, the *Drunken Faun*, the *Mercury in repose*, the *wrestlers*, busts of princes, philosophers and poets, the frightened *deer* and, amongst the marbles, the statue of the orator *Aeschines*. Beyond the peristyle to the west a long gravelled avenue led to the rotunda of the open belvedere, raised about four metres above the surrounding ground and adorned with a sumptuous circular pavement in marble intarsia (now in the Picture Gallery of the Naples Museum). A subterranean aqueduct, pointed out by Weber as an admirable and ingenious piece of hydraulic engineering, fed the great tank of the peristyle, the fountains, the *nymphaea* of the Villa and the bath of the house itself.

Perhaps one day, when all that part of Herculaneum not overbuilt by the houses of Resína will have been explored, the exploration of the wealthiest and most precious villa of the ancient world will be renewed. It will not be a vain undertaking, since not a little is still to be awaited from the complete disinterment of the living quarters and the recovery of the smaller furniture of the house, those articles of furniture which in a house of such distinction cannot fail to have a real and proper artistic value.

But the 'Villa Suburbana dei Papiri', which still floods the mystery of the disinterment of Herculaneum with the great light of the discoveries made in it, was not the only large and rich patrician villa of the district. Roman and Campanian patricians frequented the sunny, salubrious slopes and the delightful shore, and during the Imperial age the noble families of the little city itself must have preferred the more tranquil and distinguished suburban residences to the increasing noise and commercialism of city life. An Emperor, Tiberius, set the example from the solitary rock hermitage of Capri. So that the greatest promises and our good fortune are bound up, as in the past, with the excavation of other suburban villas.

FIG. 9

BRONZE CANDLESTICK

ILLUSTRATIONS

I — VESUVIUS SEEN FROM THE BELVEDERE OF THE NEW EXCAVATIONS

2 — QUARTER OF THE OLD EXCAVATIONS (1875)

3 — OLD AND NEW EXCAVATIONS: SOUTH—WEST QUARTER

4 — NEW EXCAVATIONS: SOUTH--EAST QUARTER

5 — HOUSES WITH TERRACES AND VERANDAHS ON THE SOUTH FRONT

6 — THE FOUNTAIN OF NEPTUNE (DURING THE EXCAVATION)

7 – THE FIRST GREAT EXCAVATION TRENCH

8 – THE PATIENT WORK OF THE RECOMPOSITION OF MARBLE PANELS

10 – SUPPORTS AND SCAFFOLDING NECESSARY
DURING THE EXCAVATIONS

9 – A LARGE "CUNICOLO", ALONG THE AXIS
OF THE "DECUMANUS INFERIOR"

11 — A HERCULANEAN STREET: CROSS—ROADS NEAR THE " THERMAE ,,

12 — ONE OF THE MAIN ARTERIES ("V CARDO ,,)

13 — ASPECT OF A HERCULANEAN STREET

14 — ASPECT OF A HERCULANEAN STREET

15 — CASA D'ARGO: THE PERISTYLE

16 — CASA DETTA DI GALBA: THE PORTICO AND THE CRUCIFORM FOUNTAIN

17 – CASA DETTA DELL'ALBERGO: PORTICO AND GARDEN

18 – FRONTS OF HOUSES ALONG THE " IV CARDO ,,

19 — CASA DELL'ERMA IN BRONZO

20 — CASA A GRATICCIO: FAÇADE

21 — CASA A GRATICCIO: THE "ATRIUM,, COURT

22 — CASA A GRATICCIO: WINDLASS AND ROPES

23 — CASA DEL TRAMEZZO DI LEGNO: FAÇADE

24 − CASA DEL TRAMEZZO DI LEGNO: THE " ATRIUM ,,

26 – SHOP:
WOODEN CLOTH–PRESS

25 – CASA DEL TRAMEZZO DI LEGNO:
ALCOVE AND MARBLE " TRÁPEZA ,,

27 – CASA DEL TRAMEZZO DI LEGNO: THE PARTITION WITH WOODEN DOORS

28 – CASA DELLO SCHELETRO

29 – " THERMAE ,,: THE " PALAESTRA ,,

30 – " THERMAE ,,: "APODYTERIUM ,, IN THE MEN'S SECTION

97

32 – " " THERMAE,, : " " CALIDARIUM,, IN THE WOMEN'S SECTION

31 – " " THERMAE,, : " " TEPIDARIUM,, IN THE WOMEN'S SECTION

34 – CASA DI NETTUNO E ANFITRITE: SHOP

33 – CASA DI NETTUNO E ANFITRITE: FRONT

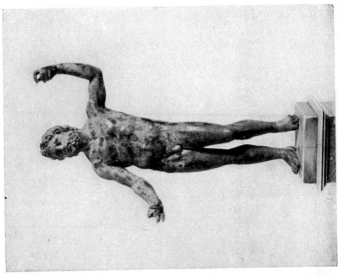

36 – CASA DI NETTUNO E ANFITRITE: STATUETTE OF JUPITER

35 – CASA DI NETTUNO E ANFITRITE: THE " NYMPHAEUM ,,

38 — CASA DEL MOBILIO: THE " LARARIUM ,,

37 — CASA DEL MOBILIO: THE " ATRIUM ,,

40 — SAMNITE HOUSE: THE " ATRIUM ,,

39 — SAMNITE HOUSE: FAÇADE

42 – WOODEN CUPBOARD AND SHRINE

41 – CASA DEL GRAN PORTALE

43 – CASA DELL'ATRIO CORINTIO: THE '' ATRIUM ,,

44 – CASA DELL'ATRIO CORINTIO: CEILING OF THE ALCOVE

45 – CASA DELL'ATRIO A MOSAICO: THE " ATRIUM ,, AND THE " TABLINUM ,,

46 – CASA DELL'ATRIO A MOSAICO: THE GARDEN

47 – CASA DELL'ATRIO A MOSAICO: THE WINDOWED PORTICO

49 – CASA DELL'ATRIO A MOSAICO:
THE PUNISHMENT OF DIRCE

48 – CASA DELL'ATRIO A MOSAICO:
THE PAINTED ALCOVE

50 – CASA DELL'ATRIO A MOSAICO: DETAIL OF WINDOWED PORTICO

51 – CASA DELL'ALCOVA: SMALL COURT

52 — SHOP (INSULA IV, N. 14)

53 — " THERMOPOLIUM ,,

54 — CASA DEI CERVI: THE GARDEN

55 — CASA DEI CERVI: THE " PERGULA ,, AND " SOLARIUM ,,

56 – CASA DEI CERVI: THE ROOM OF THE RED WALL

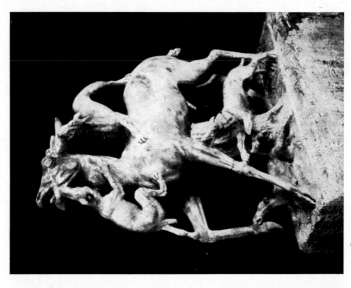

58 — CASA DEI CERVI: DEER ASSAULTED BY HOUNDS

57 — CASA DEI CERVI: SATYR WITH WINESKIN

59 — CASA DEI CERVI: CUPIDS PLAYING

60 — CASA DEI CERVI: CUPIDS AS ARMOURERS

61 – THE LARGE BUILDING OF "INSULA ORIENTALIS II,,

62 – THE GREAT VESTIBULE OF " INSULA ORIENTALIS II ,,

63 – HOUSES OF " INSULA ORIENTALIS I ,,

65 – " PISTRINUM ,,: THE OVEN

64 – " PISTRINUM ,,: BAKEHOUSE AND MILL

66 – CASA DELLA GEMMA: THE " ATRIUM ,,

67 – CASA DEL RILIEVO DI TELEFO: MARBLE " OSCILLA ,,

68 – CASA DEL RILIEVO DI TELEFO : THE " ATRIUM ,,

69 – CASA DEL RILIEVO DI TELEFO: THE ROOM WITH MARBLE DECORATION

○ — DESCENT FROM THE CITY TOWARDS THE ANCIENT SHORE OF HERCULANEUM

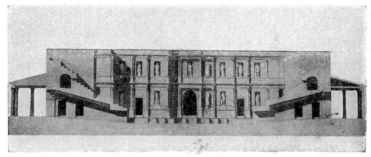

71 — THEATRE: RECONSTRUCTION OF THE " SCAENA ,, (MARZOIS)

72 — THEATRE: " PROSCAENIUM ,, AND " PULPITUM ,,

LIST OF ILLUSTRATIONS

Resina, Portici and Herculaneum 6
General plan of the ancient city. 11
Casa dell'atrio a mosaico 27
Ground–plan of the *Thermae* . . 37
Casa dei Cervi 60
Plan of the Theatre 69
Plan of the *Villa suburbana dei papiri* 72
Fragments of Herculanean papyri 75
Bronze candlestick 77
Vesuvius seen from the Belvedere
  of the new excavations 81
Quarter of the old excavations
  (a. 1875) 81
Old and new excavations: south-
  west quarter 82
New excavations: south–east quar-
  ter 83
Houses with terraces and veran-
  dahs on the south front . . . 83
The fountain of Neptune (during
  the excavation) 83
The first great excavation trench 84
The patient work of the recompo-
  sition of marble panels . . . 84
A large *cunicolo* along the axis of
  the *decumanus inferior* 85
Supports and scaffolding necessary
  during the excavations 85
A Herculanean street: cross–roads
  near the *Thermae* 85
One of the main arteries (*V cardo*) 86
Aspects of a Herculanean street . 87
Casa d'Argo: the Peristyle . . . 88
Casa detta di Galba: The Portico
  and the cruciform fountain . . 88

Casa detta dell'Albergo: Portico
  and garden 89
Fronts of houses along the *IV
  cardo* 89
Casa dell'Erma in bronzo . . . 90
Casa a graticcio: façade 91
Casa a graticcio: the *atrium* court 92
Casa a graticcio: Windlass and
  ropes 92
Casa del tramezzo di legno: façade 93
Casa del tramezzo di legno: the
  atrium 94
Casa del tramezzo di legno: alcove
  and marble *trapeza* 95
Shop: wooden cloth–press . . . 95
Casa del tramezzo di legno: the
  partition with wooden doors . 96
Casa dello Scheletro 96
Thermae: the *Palaestra* 97
Thermae: *apodyterium* in the
  men's section 97
Thermae: *tepidarium* in the wo-
  men's section 98
Thermae: *calidarium* in the wo-
  men's section 98
Casa di Nettuno e Anfitrite:
  front 99
Casa di Nettuno e Anfitrite:
  shop 99
Casa di Nettuno e Anfitrite: the
  nymphaeum 100
Casa di Nettuno e Anfitrite sta-
  tuette of Jupiter 100
Casa del mobilio: the *atrium* . . 101
Casa del mobilio: the *lararium* 101

Samnite House: façade 102

Samnite House: the *atrium* . . 102

Casa del gran portale. 103

Wooden cupboard and shrine. . . 103

Casa dell'atrio corintio: the *atrium* 104

Casa dell'atrio corintio: ceiling of the alcove 104

Casa dell'atrio a mosaico: the *atrium* and the *tablinum* . . . 105

Casa dell'atrio a mosaico: the garden 105

Casa dell'atrio a mosaico: the windowed Portico 106

Casa dell'atrio a mosaico: the painted alcove 107

Casa dell'atrio a mosaico: the punishment of Dirce 107

Casa dell'atrio a mosaico: detail of windowed portico 108

Casa dell'alcova: small Court . . 108

Shop (insula IV, n. 14) 109

Thermopolium 109

Casa dei Cervi: the garden . . . 110

Casa dei Cervi: the *pergula* and *solarium* 110

Casa dei Cervi: the room of the red wall 111

Casa dei Cervi: Satyr with wineskin 112

Casa dei Cervi: Deer assaulted by hounds 112

Casa dei Cervi: Cupids playing . 113

Casa dei Cervi: Cupids as armourers 113

The large building of *Insula orientalis II* 114

The great vestibule of *Insula orientalis II* 115

Houses of *Insula orientalis I* . . . 115

Pistrinum: bakehouse and mill . . 116

Pistrinum: the oven 116

Casa della Gemma: the *atrium* . 117

Casa del rilievo di Telefo: marble *oscilla* 117

Casa del rilievo di Telefo: the *atrium* 118

Casa del rilievo di Telefo: the room with marble decoration . 118

Descent from the cyti towards the ancient shore of Herculaneum 119

Theatre: Reconstruction of the *scaena* (Mazois) 120

Theatre: *proscaenium* and *pulpitum* 120

INDEX

Ala, alae 45
Alcove 29, 42, 63
Alcubierre 8, 68
Amazone (ermes of) 74
Cupids (paintings of) 61
Apodyterium 36, 38
Apollon (painting of) 45
Apotheca 30
Appius Claudius Pulcher . . . 70
Athena promachos (statue of) . 76
Atrium, corynthian 48
Atrium, tetrastyle 35
Atrium, testudinate 34, 59
Atrium, tuscan 32, 35
Atthis (statue of) 32
Bacchantes (paintings of) 46
Balbus (M. Nonius) 66, 70
Balteus 69
Bases (funerary) 66
Basilica 48, 70
Baths (see thermae) 35, 66
Bourbon (Charles of) 8
Bradisysmus 6
Calidarium 36, 38
Capitals 50, 61, 71
Cardines 12
Catillus 54
Caupona (shop) 55
Cavea 69, 70
Cicero 5, 73
City (the) and the monuments . 10
City area 12
Cross (emblem of) 46
Cubicula 28, 31, 32

Cumae 6
Cunei 69
Daedalus (painting of) 46
Dancers (statues of) 76
Decumani 12, 13
Decumanus inferior . . . 24, 33, 57
Decumanus maximus 48
Deer (group of) 59
Diaeta 42, 61
Diana, bathing (painting) 28
Dionysius of Halicarnassus . . . 5
Dirce (punishment of) 28
Discoveries (history of the) . . 8
Districtarium 38
Dolia 57
Doriphorus (ermes of) 74
Dyeing–shops 55, 56
Eatables 23, 41
Elboeuf (Prince of) 6, 67
Earthquake of 62 A. D. 7
Eruption 7
Europa (rape of) 40
Exedra 25, 28, 51
Fauces 31, 32, 34, 40
Faun (statues of) 76
Fistula 12, 57
Floors (upper) 15
Forms (constructional) 14
Fountain of Hercules 48
Fountain of Neptune 57
Fountain on the cardo IV . . . 44
Fountain on the cardo V 57
Forum 48
Frigidarium 36, 38

Galba (bust of) 24
Galleries (underground) ,8 19, 20, 53
Gemmarius 55
Gorgon (mask of) 44
Hercules 5
Hercules (statue of) 61
Hortus 50
House of the " Albergo ,, . . . 24
House of the " Alcova ,, ... 28
House of Argo 22
House of Aristides 22
House of the " Atrio corinzio . . 48
House of the " Atrio a mosaico . 26
House of the " due Atrii ,, . . . 34
House of the " Bel cortile ,,. . . 44
House of the " Bicentenario ,, . . 45
House of the " Cervi ,.. 59
House of the " Erma di bronzo . 27
House of Galba 24
House of the " Gemma ,, . . . 62
House of the " Genio ,, ... 23
House of the " giardino ,, . . . 50
House of the " gran portale ,,. . 50
House " a graticcio ,, ... 30
House of the " mobilio carboniz-
    zato ,, ... 41
House of the " mosaico di Nettuno
    e Anfitrite ,, ... 42
House of the " Rilievo di Telefo ,, 58
House of the " sacello in legno ,, 49
House of the " Salone nero ,, . . 39
House " Sannitica ,, ... 40
House of the " Scheletro ,, . . . 35
House of the " Stoffa ,, ... 58
House of the " telaio ,, ... 4
House of the " tramezzo di le-
    gno ,, ... 31
House Ins. IV, No. 5–6–7 . . 28
House Ins. IV, No. 8–9 30
House Ins. V, No. 11-12. . . . 45
Imagines maiorum 46

Impluvium . . . 26, 32, 35, 45, 49
Insula 10, 12, 21
Io and Argus (painting) 24
Inscriptions 7
Jupiter 43
Labrum 36, 38
Lanarius 33
Lararium 42, 47, 55
Lares 31, 45, 49, 55
Latrine 54, 56, 62
Loom 43
Lucius Annaeus Mammianus Rufus 67
Marina Gate 66
Mars (painting of) 46
Mater Deum (temple of) . 7, 20, 53
Meta 54
Mosaic (decoration) . . . 26, 34, 43
Natatio 54
Neapolis 12
Neptune and Anphitrite (mosaic of) 43
Nymphaeum 34, 43
Nuceriae 11
Numisiu (architect) 67
New excavations 18, 24
Oceanis 61
Oecus corinthius 63
Old excavations 22
Oponte 5
Opus craticium 30, 57
Opus reticulatum 22
Opus sectile 46, 59, 67
Opus tectorium 31
Opus segmentatum 36
Osci 6
Oscillum 63
Ostia 15, 51
Oven 51, 55
Palaestra (ins. orient. II) 53
Palaestra (Thermae near the
    Forum) 38
Pan (painting of) 42

Papyri 19, 74
Pasiphae (painting of) 46
Paul (holy) 46
Pergula 59
Peristyle 22, 24, 64, 78
Philodemos 76
Piscina 24, 54
Piso (Lucius Calpurnius) . . . 73
Pistrinum 54
Pomerium 66
Pompeii 13
— constructional forms 14
— eruption 7
— Forum 48
— history 6
— Marina Gate 12
— oscilla 63
— population 12
— satyr with the wineskin . . . 59
— technique of the excavations . 19
Population 12
Portico 26, 59
Portrait-bust 24
Praefurnium 37, 39
Procurator 47
Pulpitum 71
Quadriga (bronze) 14
Quadriga (reliefs with) 63
Resína 5
Samnites 6
Satyrs (painting of) 46
Satyr with the wineskin (statue of) 59
Shops of the insula II 23
Shops of the insula III 33

Shops of the insula IV . . . 56, 7
Shops of the insula V 47
Sisenna 5
Solarium 61
Sphaeristerium 40
Stabulum 54, 64
Strabo. 5, 73
Sudatio 38
Sulla 6
Tablets (wax) 21
Tablinum . . 26, 32, 40, 42, 45, 46
Talephus (relief of) 64
Teophrastos 5
Tepidarium 36, 38
Theatre 67
Thermae (suburban) 66
Thermae (in the city) 35
Termopolium 23
Textores 41
Torcularium 33
Tribunalia 69
Triclinium 28, 43, 57
Triton (mosaics with) . . . 36, 38
Vega (La) Francesco . . . 9, 10, 68
Venus 44
Venuti (de) 63
Vespasianus 7, 53
Victories (capitals with) 50
Villa dei Papiri 71
Vitruvius 30
Waldstein Charles 9
Weber Charles 9, 71
Wood (carbonized) . . . 26, 31, 41
Wrestlers (group of) 76

GENERAL INDEX

FOREWORD 3
PRACTICAL INFORMATION 4
HISTORICAL NOTE 5
   THE ERUPTION 7
   HISTORY OF THE DISCOVERIES 8
THE CITY AND ITS MONUMENTS 10
CONSTRUCTIONAL FORMS AND DEVELOPMENT IN HERCU-
   LANEUM 14
THE NEW EXCAVATIONS 18
TECHNIQUE AND ADMINISTRATION OF THE EXCAVATIONS . 19
DESCRIPTION OF THE LOCALITY 21

OLD EXCAVATIONS

INSULA II 22
   CASA DI ARISTIDE (*Insula II, n. 1*) 22
   CASA D'ARGO (*Insula II, n. 2*) 22
   CASA DETTA DEL GENIO (*Insula II, n. 3*) 23
   HOUSE AND SHOPS (*Insula II, n. 4–8*) 23
INSULA VII 24
   HABITATIONS OF *Insula VII* 24

NEW EXCAVATIONS

INSULAE III AND IV ALONG THE CARDO IV 24
   CASA DEL COSIDDETTO ALBERGO (*Insula III, n. 19*) 24
   CASA DELL'ATRIO A MOSAICO (*Insula IV, n. 1–2*) 26
   CASA DELL'ERMA DI BRONZO (*Insula III, n. 16*) 28
   CASA DELL'ALCOVA (*Insula IV, n. 3–4*) 29
   HOUSE (*Insula IV, n. 5–6–7*) 29
   HOUSE (*Insula IV, n. 8–9*) 30
   CASA A GRATICCIO (*Insula III, n. 13–14–15*) 30
   CASA DEL TRAMEZZO DI LEGNO (*Insula III, n. 11–12*) . . . 31
   SHOPS 33
   CASA DELLO SCHELETRO (*Insula III, n. 3*) 33
INSULA VI 34
   HOUSE WITH TWO COURTYARDS 34

THE THERMAE 35
    MEN'S THERMAE (*III, cardo n. 1*) 35
    WOMEN'S BATHS 38
    HOUSE OF THE BLACK HALL (*n. 11*) 39
    SAMNITE HOUSE (*Insula V, n. 1–2*) 40
    CASA DEL TELAIO (*Insula V, n. 3–4*) 41
    CASA DEL MOBILIO CARBONIZZATO (*Insula V, n. 5*) 41
    CASA DEL MOSAICO DI NETTUNO E DI ANFITRITE (*Insula V, n. 6–7*) 42
    CASA DEL BEL CORTILE (*Insula V, n. 8*) 44
    SHOP ((*Insula V, n. 10*) 44
    HOUSE (*Insula V, n. 11–12*) 45
    SHOP WITH DWELLING (*Insula V, n. 13–14*) 45
    HOUSE OF THE BICENTENARIO (*Insula V, n. 15–16*) 45
    SHOP WITH BACK–SHOP AND DWELLING (*Insula V, n. 17–18*) 47
    SHOP (*Insula V, n. 19–20*) 47
    SHOP WITH DWELLING ON THE CORNER OF THE STREET (*Insula V, 21–22*) . . 47
THE *DECUMANUS MAXIMUS* AND THE FORUM 48
    CASA DELL'ATRIO CORINTIO (*Insula V, n. 30*) 48
    CASA DEL SACELLO IN LEGNO (*Insula V, n. 31*) 49
    CASA CON GIARDINO (*Insula V, n. 33*) 50
    CASA DEL GRAN PORTALE (*Insula V, n. 8*) 50
INSULAE ORIENTALES I ET II 51
INSULA ORIENTALIS II (*Palaestra*) 52
    PISTRINUM 54
    SHOP *n. 10*, HOUSE *n. 11* 56
    HOUSE *n. 12–13* 56
    SHOP *n. 15–16* 57
    PUBLIC FOUNTAIN 57
    HABITATION AND SHOP *n. 17–18* 57
    CASA DELLA STOFFA *n. 19–20* 58
    CASA DEI CERVI (*Insula IV, n. 21*) 59
INSULA ORIENTALIS I 62
    CASA DELLA GEMMA (*Insula orientalis I, n. 1*) 62
    CASA DEL RILIEVO DI TELEFO (*Insula orientalis n. 2–3*) 63
SUBURBAN QUARTER 65
    BASES DEDICATED TO M. NONIUS BALBUS 66
    SUBURBAN BATHS 66
THE THEATRE 67
APPENDIX 71
    THE VILLA SUBURBANA DEI PAPIRI 71

JACOPO BASSANO

Comment by PIETRO ZAMPETTI

It is some time now since Jacopo Bassano, the famous Venetian painter of country scenes, aroused new interest among critics and general public. In the course of the centuries he has often been confused with his many sons and a host of imitators. But more recently a careful study of his works, which culminated in the interesting exhibition dedicated to him in Venice last year, has made it possible to arrive at a new assessment of the painter. He is now considered one of the greatest artist of Venetian painting of the XVI century, together with Titian, Lotto, Veronese and Tintoretto.

The Istituto Poligrafico dello Stato has now published all the finest works of this artist under the supervision of Pietro Zampetti, Director of Venetian Exhibitions, in one volume. There are eighty–six colour plates besides numerous reproductions in black and white. The leading museums in Europe and America, among them the Royal Collection at Hampton Court, the National Gallery in Washington, the Kunsthistorisches Museum in Vienna and the Bassano City Museum have collaborated in their selection.

The text is clear and is based on modern criteria of criticism. The artistic development of the painter is traced, his complex personality is detached from the blurred background of the Bassano family name and the fundamental characteristics of a man, highly sensitive to the culture of his times, are fully brought out. Above all he is portrayed as the happy poet of his own countryside and the lyrical interpreter of the humble whom he exalted in his numerous Nativities which are among the loveliest and most moving of their kind.

The volume is $9 \times 11^{1}/_{2}$ inches and consists of 84 pages of text with 19 illustrations, followed by 86 colour plates. Full–chot binding with gold lettering. The wrapper is of hand–made " Fabriano ., paper with a colour plate (1958).

Italian edition Lit. **15.000**
English edition Lit. **16.500**

ISTITUTO POLIGRAFICO DELLO STATO
LIBRERIA DELLO STATO - Piazza G. Verdi, 10 - ROMA